D0086065

A Street Officer's
Guide to

REPORT WRITING

by

Frank Scalise

with

Douglas Strosahl

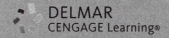

DELMAR
CENGAGE Learning®

Australia • Brazil • Japan • Korea • Mexico • Singapore • Spain • United Kingdom • United States

DELMAR
CENGAGE Learning·

A Street Officer's Guide to Report Writing, First Edition

Frank Scalise with Douglas Strosahl

Vice President, Career and Professional Editorial: Dave Garza

Director of Learning Solutions: Sandy Clark

Senior Acquisitions Editor: Shelley Esposito

Managing Editor: Larry Main

Senior Product Manager: Anne Orgren

Editorial Assistant: Diane Chrysler

Vice President, Career and Professional Marketing: Jennifer Baker

Marketing Director: Deborah S. Yarnell

Senior Marketing Manager: Mark Linton

Marketing Coordinator: Erin DeAngelo

Senior Director, Education Production: Wendy Troeger

Production Manager: Mark Bernard

Senior Content Project Manager: Kara A. DiCaterino

Art Direction: Riezebos Holzbaur

Library of Congress Control Number: 2011934998

ISBN-13: 978-1-111-54250-4

ISBN-10: 1-111-54250-3

Delmar
5 Maxwell Drive
Clifton Park, NY 12065-2919
USA

Cengage Learning is a leading provider of customized learning solutions with office locations around the globe, including Singapore, the United Kingdom, Australia, Mexico, Brazil, and Japan. Locate your local office at: **international.cengage.com/region**

Cengage Learning products are represented in Canada by Nelson Education, Ltd.

To learn more about Delmar, visit **www.cengage.com/delmar**

Purchase any of our products at your local college store or at our preferred online store **www.cengagebrain.com**

Notice to the Reader

Printed in the United States of America
1 2 3 4 5 6 7 15 14 13 12 11

The skill of writing is to create a context in which other people can think.

Edwin Schlossberg

Writing well means never having to say, "I guess you had to be there."

Jef Mallett,
Frazz, 07-29-07

CONTENTS

CHAPTER 1

And Away We Go • 1

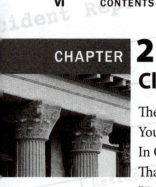

CHAPTER **2**

Clear • 21

CHAPTER **3**

Concise • 73

CHAPTER **4**

Complete • 92

CHAPTER **5**

Accurate • 113

CHAPTER 6

Conclusion • 150

AN INTRODUCTION

by Chief Anne Kirkpatrick

Photo courtesy of M. J. Rose Images.

Chief Anne Kirkpatrick, Spokane Police Department.

When Captain Frank Scalise approached me last year about writing an introduction for his new book that he and Officer Doug Strosahl were coauthoring on report writing, I was honored. But I must admit that I also thought, "Well, this will be a snoozer!" I knew that Frank was a "real" author and had published several novels. I've read one of them. Of course, the book I ventured into was action-packed, police-oriented fiction and I knew early on that Frank really had talent for writing, but again—a book about *report writing*?

I have been a police officer for almost 29 years, so I have read my share of police reports. Now, as a beady-eyed administrator, I have also read tons and tons of e-mails, memos, and administrative reports. I am also a lawyer, so I have a high tolerance for the drab and mind-numbing reading of legal documents, briefs, and case law. Overall, I love to read and I have a great appreciation for good wit and writers who can make their thoughts flow. I must admit, I prefer a good biography to fiction; nevertheless, I want to be entertained when I read.

I cannot tell you how pleasantly surprised I was in reading *A Street Officer's Guide to Report Writing*. I had emotionally prepared to hunker down to make myself read a book on report writing, and I was hooked 15 pages into the book. Captain Scalise and Officer Strosahl have managed to turn a typically dry and boring topic into a lively, realistic, and fun way to remember the "four pillars" to effective report writing.

I wholeheartedly embrace their approach that the job is never done until the report is done, but I also so much appreciate that your number one job is to be safe out there!

Enjoy this soon-to-be-a-pillar-of-all-report-writing books ever written!

Anne E. Kirkpatrick
Chief of Police, Spokane, Washington

FOREWORD

by Thomas "Tad" Hughes, Director, Southern Police Institute

Hawthorne noted that "Easy reading is damn hard writing." The difficulty of becoming an accomplished writer in any field is well known. Consider the possible interpretations of the following newspaper headlines: "Police Begin Campaign to Run Down Jaywalkers," "Juvenile Court to Try Shooting Defendant," and "Prosecutor Releases Probe into Undersheriff." Clearly, even professional writers can have difficulty clearly communicating their ideas.

In few professional arenas are writings more important than in law enforcement. Police reports supply accurate and relevant information necessary for case processing. As such, police reports shape the lives of victims, offenders, and criminal justice actors. Moreover, police reports are utilized by police administrators, media, and the courts for accountability purposes. Indeed, we are in an era of "American policing" in which police documentation has taken on an increased relevance. The management accountability model of COMPSTAT relies heavily upon the initial information collected by responding officers. Similarly, the related practices of evidence-based policing and intelligence-based policing require the analysis of timely and accurate information to evaluate and coordinate police efforts. In short, police reports facilitate an understanding of crime and criminality in a jurisdiction.

Despite this critical role in case resolution and in larger police paradigms, few tasks are viewed as more painful than report writing. Regardless of when they are completed during a shift, the task of writing reports removes officers from the world of pragmatic action and redirects them to a task of administrative recording. Scalise and Strosahl have performed an important service to those in law enforcement; they have effectively communicated the core ideas of good report writing with numerous examples and timely humor.

Conveying to officers what makes a "good" report and providing officers with the tools necessary for improvement of their report writing skills are critical educational tasks. The authors ensure that the four core attributes of strong police writings are clearly conveyed to future and current police practitioners. The characteristic of clarity is the first to be discussed. Clarity in documentation ensures that police reports are understandable to a variety of consumers. The concept involves a variety of factors from the general appearance of the report to the word selected and how the report is organized.

Next, the authors work to ensure that those who write police reports keep them "short and sweet." Some reports are longer simply because time was not taken to make them shorter. A concise report avoids clutter, while containing a full explanation of an incident. All the necessary information is included, but the desire to include additional information is successfully resisted.

Although being concise is critical, officers must be sure that their reports are complete. Documentation that does not contain relevant information may artificially limit the potential of the criminal justice system to understand both individual crimes and trends in criminality. Police officers who master the process of report writing find the clear balance between being concise and being complete.

The last core requirement of good report writing is accuracy. Documentation must reflect the true facts of the case. An accurate report is a correct and specific reflection of an incident. Officer opinions are easily identified. This level of accuracy is critical because other people will consume the report and interpret its meaning. During this process, the reader always brings some of his own perspective. Accuracy in a report limits the amount of personal interpretation a reader can interject into his understanding of an incident. As such, accuracy ensures that the foundation for future decision making by the criminal justice system is based on the facts and not the interpretations of those who consume reports.

Reading this book has reaffirmed my commitment to continually improve my writing. The only way to ensure improvement is to diligently review one's work and accept critiques. While Ken Blanchard is correct in noting that "feedback is the breakfast of champions," it's typically not a

Happy Meal. Officers who read this book and understand the four main pillars that support strong report writing have started on a journey to becoming better writers. Those who review their work to ensure that it is clear, concise, complete, and accurate will most assuredly become better report writers. Perhaps more importantly, those who rely upon their efforts will have better information to make decisions that have an impact on the nature of crime and disorder in their communities.

Thomas "Tad" Hughes
Director, Southern Police Institute

PREFACE: A GREETING

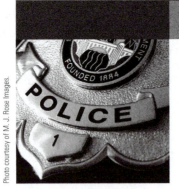

What Are You Getting Yourself Into?

Hello. I'm Frank. I will be your guide on this little foray into the exciting world of police report writing (with some help from my lovely assistant, Doug).

Who are we? Well, we'll get to that shortly, but first let me ask, Who are you? Now, I'm guessing that you are probably a new police officer[1] who wants to improve your report writing skills. Or maybe you are a student in college, hoping and planning to break into the field. Or you might be a student police officer attending the police academy somewhere. In any event, you're planning on needing to (or *getting* to,[2] depending on your attitude) write police reports. Doug and I are here to help you with that.

I will definitely do my utmost to get as much valid, important information across to you as possible, but don't expect a dry textbook here, folks. I'm hoping that you enjoy the time you spend holding this book and reading its pages. So there may be some jokes, some side-bar comments, and some general irreverence— maybe even a few war stories. Otherwise, I wonder how much of the contents will truly stick in your mind.

Expect to read about the subject of report writing and law enforcement in bluntly truthful terms. Law enforcement is a profession, but it is one with edges and it deals daily with human ugliness.

---

1   Or an old salt looking for some new perspective.
2   "Getting to" because being in law enforcement is a privilege and an honor.

Police reports chronicle that ugliness. If you don't want to hear about the reality of this world, stop reading. Consider changing your major. Drop out of the academy. With all due respect to Jack Nicholson,[3] if you can't handle the truth, you probably shouldn't be looking at a career in law enforcement or corrections—which pretty much negates any need to read this book.

;-)

Except for the above instance, I won't be using emoticons. This may seem like an informal book,[4] but it isn't e-mail. If you can't get the tone or intent of what I'm saying, then either I failed to transmit the message or you failed to receive it. If I failed to transmit, that's poor writing on my part. I shouldn't get to use a crutch like a little smiley face or a wink to make up for a lack of writing skill.

Of course, if you failed to receive, that's on you. Try again, as many times as you like, because admission is only charged once.

What's different about this report writing book when compared to all the others out there? Well, I haven't read all the others, so I can't tell you for certain. I do know that they were likely written by one of two kinds of people. Some were written by professors of English or social sciences who have never worked the street. While they might be chock-full of great technical advice on writing, my guess is most of them are lacking on the "job" side of the house.

The other group consists of cops or former cops who, like Doug and me, take an interest in the subject of report writing. Don't try to guess why. We're just sick that way. But we do bring real-life experience to the table, which is pretty valuable stuff. Luckily, we're both somewhat educated, so hopefully we can bridge that contentious gap between the academic and the street.

In this book, you're going to get the straight scoop. It should read to you like we're just sitting around, talking about report writing. Granted, that probably only takes place in an educational environment or some similar training setting. So let's consider this like a classroom. With the door closed. And just us. No stuffed-shirt types

3   "You can't handle the truth" was a climactic line delivered by Jack Nicholson in the film *A Few Good Men*. Ironically, much of what Nicholson's character said about providing security was true and also applies to law enforcement. It just didn't justify the terrible actions his troops took in the film.

4   It definitely is.

peeking in and wondering if that really was some laughter that filtered out into the hallway. Or if that was something inappropriate, such as profanity or philosophy. Whoever's closest to the door, just flip the lock, please.

There. Just us pigeons now. And we're going to take a sometimes (OK—*usually*) boring but very important topic and hopefully make it fun.

Life is about balance. Read this book. It isn't very long. If it helps you out, great. If you find yourself needing to read another one, be it written by a professor or another cop, go right ahead. We won't be offended. As long as you like this one best.

This would be where I would insert a wink or a smiley face if I didn't have faith in you.

Beyond the Book: Companion Website

Can't get enough of this topic? Visit www.cengagebrain.com and log in to the companion website that accompanies this book to access a variety of sample blank report forms and examples of well-written reports of all stripes (burglary, assault, etc.).

Wherefore Writeth Thou?

Why would we want to write a book about report writing?

Well, why not?

OK, so maybe that's not such a great answer, even if it *did* work pretty well back in junior high.

The truth, then. The truth is that report writing is a crucial element of being a successful law enforcement professional. It's not just that it is crucial to the individual officer's success, either. The success of everyone else along the criminal justice food chain (and many outside of it) depends upon how well a law enforcement report is written. We'll expand upon this later, but think about that for a minute. Some weighty issues in this world can and will be decided based upon the work some patrol officer does at zero dark thirty in the morning. Pretty important? Yeah, I'd say so.

We'll talk some more about this, and after that, I'll wager you'll agree.

But there's another aspect to the reason Doug and I wrote this book. We know that while report writing is a critical part of being a good cop,[5] we also know how the subject gets short shrift. For the most part, people in the criminal justice field don't enjoy writing reports. They sometimes enjoy what they did that causes them to have to write the report—an arrest, a chase, that sort of thing—but few law enforcement folks actually dig writing the report. It is, as we'll discuss later, *boring*.

So we figured that it was time for a book that took an important law enforcement skill (and one that can be improved) that was generally considered boring and sex it up. Make it fun. Talk about it in a straightforward, conversational way that pulls no punches but gets the important points across. Because if you can get people to read something like that and enjoy the read, then maybe they'll learn from it and then, just maybe, they'll get to be better report writers.

And we need that.

Who's Who in This Zoo?

OK, so who the heck am I, anyway? Who is going to be talking with you for the next 50-some thousand words (with the occasional input from Doug, of course)? Who is Frank Scalise that you should read this book and maybe take the lessons as having just a little bit of merit?

Well, I've been a cop in Spokane, Washington, since 1993.[6] During that time, I've worked a lot of patrol. I spent some of that time as a reserve officer mentor and as a field training officer. Then I started getting promoted—first to corporal, then detective, then sergeant, then lieutenant, then captain, where I currently serve. At every stage, I found myself looking at reports just a little differently (and needing different things out of them), which has given me some good perspective on the subject. That's good for you, too, because I'll share those different perspectives with you to help you write a report that will stand up to the scrutiny of people from all different parts of the law enforcement community (and from outside it, too).

I started teaching at the Basic Law Enforcement Academy here in Washington (Spokane branch) in 2002. The first class I taught was Sexual

5   And by "cop," we mean police officer, deputy, agent, corrections officer, probation or parole, detective, investigator—you get the picture.

6   This came after a five-year stint in the U.S. Army, where I served in military intelligence. Go ahead. Make your jokes. Get them out of the way, because we have some work ahead of us.

Assault investigation. I made report writing an important element in this course. A year later, I took over the Report Writing curriculum. I taught both courses until 2007, when I became a lieutenant. The Report Writing course was taken over by my colleague and co-instructor, Doug Strosahl.

I've also done some course writing for a national college chain, both for on-site and online courses. In on-site courses, that essentially means that I designed the courses, the exercises, and so forth, but another instructor taught the course in the classroom. In the online courses, I wrote all of the slides that the students read while taking the course. One of the courses that I developed and wrote both on-site and online versions was Report Writing.

I'm also a published novelist and short story writer. That's an entirely different type of writing and doesn't necessarily make me any more quali- fied to talk specifically about report writing, but hopefully it gives you an idea of the rounded nature of my writing experience.

My colleague, Doug Strosahl, will contribute to this book through- out. For the sake of delivery, those contributions will be invisible, but trust me—he's out there.

Doug has been a police officer since 1998 and was a reserve officer for two years prior to that. He still works out on patrol as his primary function. This is good news for you, the reader, in that he still has that boots-on-the- ground, frontline perspective on reports. Doug has worked as a reserve offi- cer mentor and is a current field training officer. He instructs report writing at the Reserve Academy and was my co-instructor at the Basic Academy before taking the lead position in that course. He is also an adjunct professor at Spo- kane Community College, where he teaches—guess what?—Report Writing.

So there you go—now you've got our horsepower.

A Pecking Order

Listen carefully, folks. This is the voice of experience here.

Can I get a drum roll, please?

Ahem.

The number one consideration, at all times, in law enforcement is and must always be *officer safety*. Get home alive. Get your partner home alive. Every day. *Nothing* trumps that.

If anyone (and I do mean *anyone*) comes along and tells you that officer safety is important but the subject matter he is about to teach is even *more* important, immediately disregard anything he says after that. Because that person is an idiot.[7]

Get home alive. Get your partner home alive. That exists on a level all by itself. Nothing is more important. Nothing trumps it. Not *ever*.

Now, all of that said, there exists a second tier of importance in law enforcement subject matter and skills that is shared by a number of disciplines. Criminal law, for example. Criminal procedures. Interview and interrogation. All of these are critical elements to be successful in law enforcement. All are important, and no one of them is necessarily more important than the other.

Right there on that same second tier, you will also find report writing. Except for officer safety, there is nothing more critical than your report writing skills. There are some things *equally* so, such as the subjects I just mentioned, but none of them are *more* important.

So there you have it in a nutshell. This is who we are, what we bring to the table, and what we hope to accomplish.

And what is that?

To make you a better report writer.

So let's get to it.

What to Expect When You're Expecting—a Textbook

This book is not your father's textbook—but it is still a textbook. Sorta. In any event, here's what you can expect is ahead of you. We'll start in chapter one discussing what a police report is and what it isn't. We'll also detail who it is that will be reading your reports. Pay attention to that—it is important to know your audience.

Chapter Two focuses on the first pillar of an excellent report—clarity. By clarity, we mean how your report looks, how you format it, what order you put events in, the whole enchilada. We'll even get into spelling and grammar, which I am sure is the subject everyone is dying to dig into. But it's important, so we will.

Chapter Three is about being concise. Be brief but be complete. We'll show you what that means and how to do it.

---

7 Someone will want to argue this point, I'm sure. Ignore him. He's an idiot, too.

Coincidentally, Chapter Four is about being complete. In this chapter, you will learn about why something has to be in a report for it to actually "happen" and take a page from our friends in the journalism department—all in order to ensure that your report is complete.

The final pillar is accuracy, which we explore in Chapter Five. Here we discuss the different meanings of being accurate and how this is likely the most critical (and most expected) element of a police report. We'll even venture into the controversial territory of opinions before covering how imperative it is to proofread your work.

In Chapter Six, we wrap it all up. If you want to go home after that, you can. But for those with more interest in the subject, we put in some bonus features as well.

There are bonuses in this book as well. They come in the form of appendixes. In Appendix A, I will draw on my varied experiences in different law enforcement positions to lay out what it is that different consumers within your agency are likely to be looking for in your report. The purpose of this is perspective. As I mentioned earlier in this section, it is important to know your audience. If you know what someone is probably going to look for in your report, you may be well served to make sure you include it there. Otherwise, you might be subjected to the dreaded meeting with your sergeant that starts with, "I need you to write a supplemental report on what you did." Never fun. Better to anticipate and provide.

Appendix B explores other types of law enforcement written communication—e-mails, commendations, memoranda, evaluations, and so forth. If you're in the target audience of this book—a criminal justice student, an academy student, a newer officer, or a veteran officer wanting to improve report writing skills—you may not get as much out of Appendix B as you will out of the rest of the book. But if you spend any time in law enforcement (or if you promote or take a leadership position on a specialty team), you'll have occasion to write one of these documents. Appendix B will help you with that. And besides, who doesn't use e-mail these days?

Appendix C is your final exam, should you choose to take it. If you read *A Street Officer's Guide to Report Writing* with even half an eye, this should be a breeze. The answers are in Appendix D.

Lastly, Appendix E is an example of a good burglary report. Doug wrote it, just to give credit (or blame) where it is due. If you do the related exercises at the end of chapters two, three, four, and five, you should end up with something close to what Doug did in Appendix E.

ACKNOWLEDGMENTS

No one does anything alone these days. Certainly a book doesn't make it into your hands without the work of a great number of people. Before we dive into report writing, let's say a few well-earned thank-yous.

Frank's Acknowledgments

I'd like to thank: my partner and friend, Doug, for being good at exactly those two things; my wife Kristi for her constant and unequivocal support coupled with her honesty; Lonnie Schaible and Ronald Harris for helping get this book in the right hands; Shelley Esposito for being those right hands; Danielle Klahr for pinch hitting; Anne Orgren for being everything an editor is supposed to be—firm and flexible; Mike Prim for beta testing this with his students; Jerry Wood for teaching me first about police reports; every BLEA class that ever sat through my course of instruction—I learned a great deal about report writing thanks to you; the men and women of the Spokane Police Department, who are the reason I wear that patch with pride; every one of you reading this book that does (or will) serve in one of the most important, noble, sometimes thankless, professions—criminal justice. I hope this book makes your life easier.

Doug's Acknowledgments

First of all, I would like to thank Captain Frank Scalise for his dedication and commitment to this book. His wisdom, experience, and writing skills are what really made this book possible. I would also like to thank him for rekindling my passion for helping others improve their police report writing skills. I am proud to call him mentor and friend. Thank you, all of my students in BLEA and SCC for sitting through my long classes and helping me remember what it is like to be just starting out in this field. Lastly, I would like to thank Delmar Cengage Learning for believing in this book and providing the guidance to make it such a valuable resource for police officers everywhere.

Thanks to the Reviewers

Frank, Doug, and Cengage Learning would like to thank the following reviewers for their input and expertise:

Thomas Adams, Del Mar College

Kimberley K. Blackmon, Department Chair for Criminal Justice, Remington College Online Programs

Henry L. Cho, Police Sergeant, CEO, Cho Research & Consulting, LLC

Kenneth Christopher, Park University

John Edward Coratti, Director of Criminal Justice, Lamar State College–Orange, certified police academy instructor

Wes Harris, University of Phoenix

James Lauria, Pittsburgh Technical Institute, Chief of Police/ Director of Public Safety

Sharon Lubinski, Assistant Chief of Police, Minneapolis

James Scariot, Heald College

Christine Stymus, Bryant & Stratton

Lt. Michael A. Prim, Spokane Police (Retired), Department Chair CJ Program, Spokane Community College

Photo courtesy of M. J. Rose Images.

AND AWAY WE GO

WHAT IS A POLICE REPORT?

If we're going to talk about report writing, I suppose we have to start with a basic definition. What is a police report, anyway?

Simply put, a police report is how we document the work we do. Reports are normally broken into two parts: report forms and report narratives. We document all of the biographical information about a person (name, birth date, address, etc.) and specifics involving the incident (date, time, type of event) on each report we complete, and we use forms to do so. The many different forms in use vary from agency to agency. Most involve filling in boxes of some kind—not exciting, but crucial. We will briefly touch on the importance of forms in Chapters 4 and 5.

The second part of a police report is the report narrative. This is the portion of the report that your readers will be most interested in. It tells them, in your words, what happened during a specific incident. The primary focus of this book is how to effectively write the narrative of a police report.

I YAM'T WHAT I YAM'T

Now you have a basic definition of what a police report *is*. But before we go any further, let's take a look at what a police report *isn't*.

A police report isn't an essay. You are not writing to express an idea, a philosophy, or any other point. You are not trying to persuade anyone to agree with you about a subject.

That said, who remembers writing essays in high school or college? Do you remember the "bologna sandwich" structure that most English teachers taught? It goes something like this. An essay has a theme. An essay is five paragraphs long. It has three main points, each supporting the overall theme. The first paragraph (the bread) is an introduction, which introduces the concept and states the theme of the essay. Paragraphs two, three, and four support the overall theme. Each of these middle three paragraphs (the meat and cheese of the sandwich) has a single point to make in support of the main theme. The final paragraph (and the second piece of bread) is a summary and conclusion.

Did I get that right, Mr. Wilson? After all, it was 1983 that I last received formal instruction on the bologna sandwich model. I'm pretty sure I hit the broad strokes of it, though.

So if a police report isn't an essay, should you just throw out everything you learned about essay structure in school?

You wish.

Actually, there are a lot of useful elements from the old bologna sandwich that you can incorporate into police report writing. Though the purpose of the police report is completely different, the basic structure of an introduction, a body, and a conclusion remains very similar. So don't throw out your sophomore English composition textbook just yet.

Another reason it isn't an essay is simply the purpose. An essay is usually intended not only to inform but to convince or sway a person on a topic. It can be strictly opinion, it can be logic based, or it can use facts and figures to convince; but the ultimate purpose is usually to convince someone to make an informed belief—the one the author is presenting.

OK, so a police report isn't an essay. So what is it?

Well, it *isn't* a personal letter, that's for sure. The informal, rambling nature of most letters is completely inappropriate for police reports.

No one writes letters anymore, you say?

All right, I'll concede the point. *Almost* no one writes letters anymore. The world has moved on. Even soldiers overseas log on to Hotmail at the PX or something. So substitute in the word *e-mail* and the sentiment is the same. A police report is *not* an e-mail. E-mails range from formal business e-mails to informal notes; so aside from the formality of a police report, what else is the difference?

The purpose, again. The purpose of an e-mail is usually direct communication and usually intended for a single or limited audience. A police report has a target audience, but it must be accessible to lay readers, as well.

Not an essay and not a letter. What else?

A police report is certainly not a short story. For one, a short story is fiction. A police report obviously deals in facts and only real, true facts. A short story is made up. Your report should not read like a Stephen King story. Or any other, for that matter.

As long as we're talking fiction, a police report is not a newspaper article, either. This is true for a variety of reasons. For one, a police report must be true and accurate.

Oh, sorry. Does that come across as a slam on newspapers?

Well, good.

While the aspiring journalists in the audience are drawing their knives and intending to gut me in indignation, let me tell you why else a police report isn't like a newspaper article. A police report must be objective. It seems like most newspapers have an agenda. It may be a small agenda; it may be a big one. It may lean left; it may lean right. Most of the time, it isn't even the reporters themselves but the editors. But I've seen enough in my career to know this is the way of things. Events reported in the newspaper will in some way be filtered through the experience and biases of the reporter *and* the editor *and* the guy who writes the headline. Couple that with the natural deviations that occur when one person tells a story to another (and another and another) and you have an account that is something less than accurate.

The same problem exists in a law enforcement setting when it comes to the transferring of a story from one person to another, but the personal agenda part is something that *cannot* occur. As a law enforcement report writer, you simply don't have that luxury. You gave up the right to be subjective in your written work product when you signed on to be a cop.

Sorry.

Really, I am. I'm sure slinging mud and slanting everything you write is great fun. But you don't get to do that as a cop. Get used to it. It is just one of many higher standards you're going to be held to in this profession. And don't whine about it, either. You're being given great authority, so with that comes great responsibility. Don't like it? Get another job. Be a butcher, baker, or candlestick maker. Or a journalist, for example.

A police report differs from a newspaper article, too, in its purpose. A newspaper article (as opposed to an editorial) is designed to inform. So is a police report. But a police report is more focused, as there isn't any concern in a police report that a newspaper article may have for public consumption or all-round dissemination of information. A police report is more focused upon the facts concerning a police matter (generally criminal). Neat, little interesting facts that might end up in a newspaper article will never make it in a police report. The focus of the latter is on relevant matters only.

OK, enough newspaper bashing, as fun a sport as that may be at times. In reality, most journalists are just as "called" to their profession as cops are to theirs—and just as dedicated. The good ones serve an important purpose in a free society.

We've touched upon what a police report is *not*. Let's move on to what a police report actually *is*.

A police report represents your final work product.

IT IS WHAT IT IS

The first, and perhaps the most important, thing that I want you to know about what a police report is that *it is your work product*. It is how people who have never met you are going to know you. It is the basis upon which they will judge your competence.

It amazes me sometimes that a cop will bust his hump working a case, chase down leads, do an excellent read on evidence, do a crackerjack interview, nail a bad guy—and then write a lousy report. The end result of all that hard work is represented in the final police report. The fact is, the people who read this lousy report are going to be judging you and your work product based on your report. So why not do a great job? Why not at least finish it?

In the film *Young Guns II*, Emilio Estevez's character (Billy the Kid) is discussing options with his fellow outlaws. The group is outnumbered and hurt. They are dispirited and want to cut and run. So to inspire them, Billy tells the story of the three men who were sitting in a saloon playing Fantan. Someone ran up to them and said, "Hey, the world's coming to an end!" So the first man says, "Well, I best go to the mission and pray." The second one says, "Well, hell, I'm gonna go and buy me a case of Mescal and six whores." But the third one says, "Not me. I shall finish the game."

The cowboys rode back into the fray.[1]

Law enforcement isn't a career for shrinking violets. Yes, you need to have sensitivity, but you must have grit, too. If you don't, I'd recommend another career. That applies to working the street, for certain, but it applies

1   *Young Guns II*, 1990. Written by John Fusco.

to following through on writing a good report, too. Nothing is finished until it is finished, and as a cop, you never give up. And if pushing through the boredom or meticulous nature of writing a thorough police report is too much hard work for you—well, again, I'd suggest another career.

In police work, we *always* finish the game.

If the preceding doesn't motivate you to want to do it right, then look at it from a financial point of view. You have just spent thousands of dollars and more than likely a lot of time preparing yourself for a career in this field. If you choose to consistently do a poor job of documenting in your reports, you will no longer have the job you worked so hard to get. Why would agencies want to employ someone who doesn't do a good job? It doesn't make sense for them financially to do so (and believe me, they do look at you for what you do for them, not for what they can do for you). They can hire someone else who will do a better job in less time—so get it right, the first time, every time.

"REPORT WRITING IS BORING."

I hear that all the time. You know what? Maybe it is. So is sitting on the perimeter of a crime scene waiting for the homicide detectives to show up. So is logging 47 pieces of found property onto the property book. And don't forget guarding a prisoner at the hospital for an entire shift while he heals up enough to be booked into jail.

I could give you about nine billion other examples.

The point is, the criminal justice field—and law enforcement, in particular—is full of things that are "boring." Police work has been described as 99 percent boredom and irritation and 1 percent sheer terror. That's not far off.

But just because something is "boring" doesn't mean it isn't *critical*. Remember, the police report is your final work product. We'll talk on this some more in a bit.

What else is a police report? It is a technical report. A technical report has a number of expectations that go along with it. One, that it will be professional. Two, that it will be accurate. And three, that there is an intended audience that generally shares some knowledge of the subject matter being reported.

Let's break these down a little further.

Professional. What does that word mean? Well, aside from the dictionary definition of one who is paid for her services, there are further implications. If someone says, "She did a professional job," what are they saying? They're saying that the job was done right, on time, in the proper context, and with an appropriate attitude.

So with that in mind, would you consider either of the following sentences from actual police reports to be professional? "She was unemployed and will probably be on welfare for the rest of her life." Or how about, "I asked him his name, and, of course, he didn't know."

Both of these sentences are clearly the result of a frustrated (and in the second instance, graveyard) officer. Before you pass judgment on that frustration, I recommend you try working the street, particularly graveyard, for five or seven years. Go to call after call involving people on welfare or disability who have enough money for beer and cigarettes but apparently not enough to feed or clothe (or supervise!) their children properly. Walk into house after house where no one has a job and everyone is on public assistance but there is a big-screen plasma TV in the living room. Meanwhile, you are dodging the piles of dog crap on the carpet that has apparently become furniture. And *then* have those same people yell at you about how they pay your salary.

Or how about this? Have everyone lie to you constantly. About everything. Deal with them lying even when the truth is right in front of them or when it would set them free.

And then try not to get a little frustrated.

It grinds on you. Trust me.

All that said, there's a time and a place to vent those frustrations. Go to the gym. Spar. Hit the bag. Play video games. Fool around with your lover. Have a beer with your patrol team at the end of the week. Take a vacation. Write a book on report writing. Do whatever, but *don't put your sarcasm in your police report*. It is unprofessional. And, as we'll discuss in a few paragraphs, a police report isn't just a record—it is a *legal, public* record.

So we've established that part of writing a professional report is having a professional attitude in that report. Quite true. It is also about doing an excellent job. That is a bigger issue to tackle and is actually the focus of this entire book, so we'll come back to that frequently.

Let's move on to *accurate*. A technical report is expected to be accurate and to use means and measurements that are generally accepted in the field.

Additionally, a technical report is usually written for others in that same field. While it should be accessible to the layperson to an extent, the fact is that it is being presented to people within the same general field as the writer.

Therefore, it is not a crime to use some technical terms. Of course, it is also not a crime to take the time to at least use those terms as a full word the first time instead of turning in five pages of acronyms. But we'll get to that.

So a police report documents your work and it is a technical report. What else?

Well, as I alluded to a few paragraphs ago, it is a legal, public record. That's something you want to remember when you put pen to paper (or more likely these days, fingers to keyboard). Your police report is an official record. It is also a public record, subject to public disclosure. It doesn't go into a vault somewhere, never to be seen again. Citizens and media can and are accessing police reports more often all the time. You should write every word fully expecting that a million people might read it, just as you should conduct yourself on the street as if you're being videotaped constantly. After all, both possibilities are quite real.

As a legal, public record, your report will be relied upon by other people within the field. We'll talk some more about this in the next section.

WHO READS THIS STUFF?

So a quality police report documents the work that you did. And you're going to be judged on the quality of that report by people who have never met you. Someone is going to rely on your report for accurate information. Who are those people? Let's take a look at a partial list together and break it down a little bit.

- **Supervisors**
  - Usually the very first person that is going to see (and judge) your report is your immediate supervisor. This is the person who writes your performance reviews and approves applications for schools and specialty assignments, not to mention the all important vacation schedule. Basically, this is your boss. Do you think you might want to turn in a quality report?
- **Other Officers**
  - At times, another officer might review your report. There are a plethora of reasons this might occur. For example, the main report was the other officer's and you wrote an additional (or supplemental) report covering what you did in support of her investigation. Or an officer might read your report later because she is dealing with the same person or situation and wants some background. You want to look good to your fellow cops, right?

Often, it is your immediate supervisor who will be the first one to review your report.

Another consideration is that an officer may come across someone you had probable cause (PC) for the night before and can arrest the person based on that PC—if your report is good. Last, there may be an instance in which an officer from another jurisdiction is investigating something that relates to your report in some way. In that case, not only will your report reflect directly upon you, it will likely cause the officer from another agency (which could be clear across the country) to form an opinion about your entire agency. (Is that fair? We'll talk about that in a minute).

- Your field training officer also fits into this category. This person will be reading and analyzing every detail of your report to make sure you have it right. If you haven't, then yes—you will be doing it over.

● **Case Screeners/Crime Analysts**
  - In most agencies, reports are funneled through some sort of case screening process that determines if cases should be sent to the investigative division for follow-up consideration. Also, in many midsized and larger agencies, a team (or maybe just one person, depending on the agency) reviews incoming reports looking for crime trends. A quality report helps make this process much smoother.

● **Detectives**
  - If your report involves an investigation with follow-up potential, it might find its way into the hands of a detective. That detective is going to review your report with a critical eye, because she is going to have to conduct an investigation based on that report.

- I was a detective myself, so I can vouch for this: The first thing that almost every detective does when she receives a new case file is open it up and look down at the bottom of the report form to see who wrote it. This is so he knows whether he'll need a second cup of coffee and an aspirin before starting to read it. This may seem harsh, but the detective has to rely on what is in the incident report to do his job. Well, to *start* it, anyway. Officers quickly develop a deserved reputation regarding the quality of their reports—both good *and* bad.

- **Prosecutors**
  - Though the prosecutor in large felony cases will likely get the entire package of reports from the detective, some prosecutors (in misdemeanor cases, for example) may get the case straight away, based on your arrest. That prosecutor is going to have to meet certain legal criteria to successfully prosecute the case. A prosecutor's standard for success in trial (beyond a reasonable doubt) is considerably higher than yours to arrest (PC).
  - A quality report outlining the case in all its detail makes a prosecutor happy. And don't you want prosecutors to be happy? After all, they are the ones trying to turn your arrest into a conviction so that the criminal you arrested actually pays some form of penance for the crime—instead of being released to go out and do more crime.

- **Defense Attorneys**
  - Ah, yes. The vile ones.[2] These are the men and women who will defend in court the criminal you arrested. How will they go about it? Well, there's a saying in legal defense circles. Goes like this. If the facts are on your side, argue the facts. If the facts are not on your side, argue the investigation. And if the investigation was a good one, impugn the cops. Anyone who watches Court TV will see this on display time and time again.

2 Cops generally despise defense attorneys, especially early in their law enforcement career. As time passes, though, you realize that they do provide a vital function. Like any other group of people, there are honorable ones and there are dishonorable ones. I think that one reason for the dislike cops feel for defense attorneys is simply because the attorney points out the mistakes we make. Of course, defending criminals we caught red-handed doesn't help, either. A guy I play hockey with is a defense attorney and if I ever start ramping up on him over defending obviously guilty people, he counters with, "Hey, you can't convict them without a defense attorney."

- Now, let's imagine you wrote a poor report. This opens things up to ambiguity and uncertainty, which is all a good defense attorney needs in order to plant the seeds of reasonable doubt in a jury's mind. And that's all a jury needs to acquit.
- One more thing on defense attorneys. The first time you spend an uncomfortable half hour on the witness stand getting grilled by one, having your every error pointed out to you and examined in detail, you will be utterly convinced of the need for a quality report. Every officer that has experienced that particularly lovely time has told me how much it sucked. I believe them. Even when you did a good job and wrote a good report, cross-examination by a good defense attorney is no picnic. But if you wrote a good one, your report will be your ace in the hole.

● **Victims**

- The events in your report may be one of a dozen similar events you wrote about that month. But to the victim, that event is of paramount concern. It may be the only time in her life she was ever victimized and one of the few times she ever interacted with the police. She will probably get a copy of your report and she will read it. What do you want her to see?

● **Suspects**

- Many suspects actively participate in their own defense. They read the case reports and feed information to their attorney. Sometimes they are less than truthful.[3] If your report is vague on any matter, it may become a crucial point at trial. The possibility even exists that a less than truthful defendant may weave her explanation of events around those ambiguities in your report.

● **News Media**

- Some agencies enjoy a good relationship with the media in their community, while others have a contentious one. In either event, the media may request and receive copies of police reports under public disclosure laws. If you wrote a poor report, do you want to see an excerpt from it on the front page of the evening edition? Moreover, do you want the facts of the case misrepresented because your report was vague?

---

3 OK, *frequently* they are less than truthful.

● **Probation/Parole Officers**
  - These individuals will sometimes make decisions about revocation based on your report. A clearly written, detailed report makes their decision much easier. I think we can all agree that we should be helping these folks out. I mean, once the bad guys are in jail, let's try to keep them there.

● **Child Protective Services/Social Services**
  - Many child and social services agencies are interested in your report to help them with their own investigations. Police personnel often go to a residence many times prior to the social worker ever being notified of a problem. A well-written report detailing the police activities involving these clients will help a social worker provide the right services or make a weighty decision like whether or not to place a child in foster care.

● **Police Brass**
  - Rest assured, if an event of any magnitude occurs, the entire chain of command will be reading all of the reports pertaining to the case. Do you want your chief or sheriff reading a sloppy report or one in which you decided to make a wise crack? Trust me, they won't be impressed or amused. And because you probably don't have a lot to do with them on a daily basis, that report might just be what forms the basis of their opinion of you as a cop. As Doug Strosahl has pointed out to me on more than one occasion, once some people are promoted, they tend to lose the ability to see the humor in patrol work and forget what it's really like to walk a beat.[4]

---

4   Doug makes a good point. I remember a situation in which a deer got caught in a citizen's fence out on the edge of the city. It thrashed around, making noise and getting cut up pretty good. This drew the attention of a coyote, who hovered around about 30 yards away, waiting for the deer to expire or get weak enough that he could begin to dine. This, of course, made the deer thrash even more. When the citizen saw this, she called the police. Cops arrived, assessed the situation, and quickly recognized that the deer was dying, so they euthanized it. This, of course, upset the citizen, who called in a complaint the next day because of the traumatic experience (and the fact that animal control never showed up to pick up the carcass and all the kids had to walk past the bloody corpse of Bambi on the way to school). Because he discharged his firearm, the officer had to write a report. Because the citizen complained, the brass read the report. The final lines of the report read: "I placed the euthanized deer near the roadway for animal control to pick up. The coyote, however, remains at large." I laughed when I read that. My boss at the time was less than amused and pretty much thought that officer was a smart alec (he is, but in a good natured way—usually self-deprecating—and he's a damn fine street cop).

They (being a captain now, I am forced to say "we") definitely won't find a subpar report about a major incident to be an acceptable job.

- **Internal Affairs**
  - Oops. Someone complained about something you did. Now an Internal Affairs (IA) investigator has to look into the matter. First stop? Your report. A quality (and complete—we'll talk about that in greater detail later) report is crucial here. What if there are exculpatory facts with regard to the misdeed you are accused of but they aren't in the report? If something occurred that unquestionably shows you are innocent of the accusation but you didn't record it at the time, your "convenient" recollection after the fact of this event that is not in the report will seem self-serving at best.
  - On another note, most IA investigators started out as cops. They know that a good number of complaints are bogus and that another large chunk of them are simply perception issues. A good police report (and a track record of good reports doesn't hurt, either) by an officer can turn a formal complaint into a mere inquiry in a hurry. At worst, it ensures that those who must sit in judgment on this complaint will have a complete picture to work with.

- **Insurance Companies**
  - When you work up a collision report or investigate a burglary, there is another side to the case that law enforcement really doesn't deal with, yet we have considerable impact upon the outcome. Your police report will generally be considered the "gospel" of events. If you are writing a collision report, for instance, insurance companies who are haggling over fault and who pays whom will rely heavily upon your report. If you investigate a burglary, the victim's homeowner's insurance agent will review your report and give it a great deal of weight in making decisions about the claim. This could involve whether or not a worthy victim is properly compensated, or it could result in an insurance investigator catching on to a fraudulent claim.

- **You (Later, in Court)**
  - Think you'll remember every detail of every call you ever go on? Think again. You'll remember them all—for about a year. Then they'll slowly start to melt into each other, and soon you'll only remember the ones that truly stand out. That is, until you re-read your report, which will spark your memory. Then you will

remember the specifics of a particular call you went on, even if it occurred years before. Didn't write a good report? Yeah, sucks to be you.

I can speak directly to a number of these roles because I have filled several of them during my career. I have been that other officer who has looked at an additional report that was supposed to contain a vital element of PC to my case and found it missing—or poorly described.

I've been that field training officer who couldn't even recognize what call the recruit was writing about when she handed me the report—even though I was there.

I've been the detective who opened the case file, looked to the bottom of the page, and groaned at the name I saw there.

I've been the supervisor trying to read a sloppily written and poorly constructed report through bleary eyes at four o'clock in the morning. Or the investigative sergeant thinking to myself, "How can I justify assigning this mess to a detective?"

I've sat on cases with prosecutors and watched them judge an officer based partially or wholly on the police report she wrote. I've seen defense attorneys carve up a nice section of roasted cop on the witness stand, served up by the officer's own poor report.

I've been that member of "the brass" who had to review a report because of an IA claim or a complaint, or because a collision or a use of force was involved. And when I didn't really know much about the officer from personal experience, I will confess to letting a sloppy report depicting sloppy work and poor decision making affect my opinion of the officer. I've also had exactly the opposite happen.

I have seen examples of a bad report hurting the officer, the agency, and the victim in every instance listed here—and more. I've also seen a good report make a case or save an officer.

CASE IN POINT

In 1996, I was a patrol officer assigned to the south side of the city. My partner and I were dispatched on a welfare check. The subject of this welfare check was a 1-year-old girl that a young mother was apparently looking for all around the neighborhood. The call was a bit of a mess, if I remember right, but ultimately what it came down to was that we were looking for a little girl that might be missing. Somehow (and I forget at the moment how—wish I had my report handy!), we ended up at a residence where the woman was supposed to live. We knocked at the door, which was standing open, for the longest time but got no answer. Loud music was playing inside and a man was asleep on the couch and not responding to us. Based on the exigency of the situation, we decided to go inside, make contact, and try to locate the child.

The guy was drunk and sound asleep. I remember it was difficult to wake him. The place was a disaster. Old clothing, food, and garbage everywhere. Completely unsanitary and unfit for a child.

We woke the guy up finally and told him why we were there. He turned out to be the child's father, but he didn't know where the mother or the child was. Nor was he too concerned. This was 1996, before everyone and their brother had a cell phone. So we were stuck. We checked around the house to see if the baby was there, and she wasn't.

There was, however, a marijuana grow operation in the basement—and prominent evidence of methamphetamine use, though no actual meth.

My partner and other officers kept looking for the mother while I simultaneously applied for and received a search warrant for the grow operation. After further investigation, we located the child in the care of someone only tenuously connected to the mother or father. We called the child's grandmother to come and get the child, something she was only too happy to do.

Eventually, the mother showed up at the house. She still didn't know where her kid was, but didn't ask about that. Instead, she asked about the father, who was under arrest for the marijuana grow. She even tried to take responsibility for the marijuana grow, though she clearly didn't know anything about it—not how many plants, what stage of growth they were in, or even where the grow was inside the house. Ironically, though, she did have a warrant and when I arrested her, she had methamphetamine on her. So she got her wish to go to jail after all.

Child Protective Services (CPS) came and approved temporary placement of the child with the maternal grandmother, who was quite distressed over the living conditions in the house and the supervision that wasn't happening.

In 2002, I received a subpoena from a private attorney. The grandparents in this case were suing the parents for custody of the two children (these sterling parents now had a second child). The children were still being neglected and repeatedly placed in harmful situations as a result of the continued drug use of both parents.

I had to testify to events that were six years old. I'd been promoted twice since 1996. How many other welfare checks do you think I'd been on, not to mention calls? How many reports had I written and read?

So what did I have to rely on to help me recall events? My police report, of course. Luckily, it was detailed enough to spark my memory of the entire case. Thus, I was able to testify truthfully and convincingly, along with another officer who'd arrested the parents earlier that very month for other drug offenses. I was able to recall, both from my report and memory, a number of specific details about the terrible state of the house and the irresponsible attitude of the parents.

There is a happy ending here, folks. The grandparents got the kids, and now they're in a much happier place. They get a shot in this world at having a nice life instead of what awaited them at the hands of their drug-addled parents. But what if I'd written a poor report and had to answer "I don't remember" to a lot of the attorney's important questions? He told us afterward (wrote us a thank-you letter, actually) that our detailed testimony was crucial in the outcome of the case. So if I'd written a marginal report, maybe that civil case would've turned out differently. And that would have had a profoundly negative effect on those two kids, both under age 6 at the time.

Luckily, I wrote a good report in that instance and was able to contribute to a positive outcome. You never know why you might need your report to be a good one, so make them all that way.

A TRIP TO THE FAIR

Something I already mentioned is that you will be judged by the quality of your reports. In some cases, you will be judged *strictly* by those reports.

Is that fair? Raise your hand if you think so.

OK, hands down.

Now raise 'em if you think it's not fair.

Why isn't it fair? Well, because there's more to being a cop than just report writing, isn't there? I mean, you could be a great investigator, excellent at finding every bad guy in town, and able to interview a hardened criminal and a weeping victim with equal skill. You might be the best

Photo courtesy of M. J. Rose Images.

If you want "fair," look for ferris wheels. Life isn't fair.

pursuit driver, best at defensive tactics, best shot on the firing range, and best joke teller in the entire patrol division. So how can someone look at one of your reports that is subpar and judge you *only* by that?

That's not fair at all.

Why could you say that it *is* fair? Well, because that's all that most of the readers will know of you. How else should they judge you?

Fair or not, it is reality—people *will* judge you on the quality of your reports.

Another reality is this: Even if you do catch every bad guy in town, if you can't document what one did wrong in a report that's good enough to get a conviction, what good are you to your agency, fellow officers, and community you are supposed to serve? When you put it in that context, I guess it ends up being pretty fair, after all.

Ultimately, in life, fair is something you take your kids to. It's where you can eat cotton candy and go on all the rides. Maybe ride a pony. It's not what you can expect life to be. Write a good report and you won't have to worry about it.

A QUALITY REPORT

We've talked about what a report *is,* what it *isn't,* who reads it, and whether it is fair that they judge you based on it. But why should you be interested in writing a quality report?

For one, it demonstrates a quality work product. As a law enforcement officer, it is your duty to produce a quality product. Likewise, I would hope you have enough pride in your work to want that product to be of high quality and to withstand scrutiny.

Another reason is criminal prosecution. A poor report can result in a case being dismissed (by the prosecutor or later by the judge) or lost.

Also, a good report protects the officer. An accusation against an officer may be baseless, but if the report is ambiguous on the contested point, she is at risk.

Lastly, there is the issue of accountability. We are accountable to our bosses for our work product. Ultimately, our boss is the public. The citizens we serve have the right to expect a quality report from each of us. And the public can be a hard, cold employer at times.

So then, how do you accomplish writing a quality police report? Let's see.

FOUR PILLARS

There are four pillars of quality report writing. In order to be a good police report, the document must be **clear, concise, complete** and **accurate.** Think of these as legs of a table or pillars of a building. If you remove any one and then apply the slightest pressure, the structure will fall.

Let's touch briefly on each of these pillars.

- *Clear.* Quite simply, what occurred must be communicated *clearly* to the reader.
- *Concise.* The report must *not* include irrelevant, distracting details.
- *Complete.* It must, however, include *all* relevant details.
- *Accurate.* All details within the report must be *accurately* recorded.

If the table with four legs or building with four pillars analogy isn't working for you, try this one. Imagine you've purchased a prefabricated item such as a desk or a swing set. These items come with instructions, right? And these instructions are always crystal clear and simple, no?

No?

Well, if the instructions aren't clear, you'll find yourself scratching your head, throwing things, or ending up with something resembling interpretative art of some kind instead of what you bought.

If the instructions aren't concise, you will be reading about the factory where the parts were made, who the foreman was, and what the weather was like when the item was packaged. What a waste of time that would be.

What if the instructions are not complete? Well, just try one time to skip a couple of instructions the next time you put together a bookshelf you bought at the store and see what you end up with. It won't be pretty and it won't be a bookshelf, I can guarantee you that.

Lastly, if the directions aren't accurate, you won't end up with a desk or a swing set, either. You'll have a pile of garbage, more likely—or ashes, depending upon your patience level. Because if Tab A belongs in Slot B but the directions say Slot Z, we've got trouble in River City.

The instructions to a prefab item are essential. They must be clear, concise, complete, and accurate. Likewise, your police report is a legal, professional document that must be the same.

So let's dig into the four pillars, starting with clarity.

Photo courtesy of M. J. Rose Images.

DISCUSSION POINTS

There will be exercises at the end of some of the more technical chapters, but because this chapter is about the philosophy of a police report, we decided to include some discussion points instead. These are intended as a jumping off point for you to kick around in your mind or in a classroom setting.

1. How is a police report different from an essay? How is it similar?

2. Do you believe that a police report is similar to a letter or an e-mail? Why or why not?

3. How does a police report differ from a newspaper article? What elements of a newspaper article apply to a police report?

4. In what way does a police report represent your work product?

5. Are there any legal considerations to a police report?

6. How widely is a police report viewed within the criminal justice field?

7. What entities outside of criminal justice might view a police report?

8. Do you believe it is fair that a person may judge you based solely upon one of your reports? Why or why not?

CLEAR

THE FIRST PILLAR

The first pillar of a good police report is clarity. A report must be CLEAR.

The person who reads a police report must be able to understand it. This is the first rule of communication and the first goal—to be understood. If a report is unclear, it will be difficult or impossible to proceed with a criminal investigation. Worse yet, it opens up the agency and the officer to civil lawsuits.

The very purpose of writing a report is to convey information. If the intended message is not delivered, then that endeavor is, quite simply, a failure.

So how do you make your report clear?

Writing a clear police report is as simple as this—say what you mean[1] in a way that the reader can understand it. One sure way to lose the vast majority of your readers is to write your report using "big" words. A large portion of people (sadly) in our country read at about an eighth-grade level, even those with college degrees. If you write your reports to this target audience, you are guaranteed it will be clear to everyone who reads it. This doesn't mean "dumb it down"; it simply means to consider using common wording. For example, instead of saying

> **She behaved in a very esoteric manner during my interview,**

you could simply say

> **She was acting mysterious during my interview.**

Unfortunately, any number of obstacles exist to the rather simple proposition of saying what you mean. These obstacles can be overcome, but you as the writer have to be aware of them and the impact they have on the reader. Some are visual, like neatness or format; some involve word choice; and others have to do with the format and structure of the report.

Let's break down these obstacles and how to overcome them.

---

1 Pretty much a good rule of thumb in life all the way around.

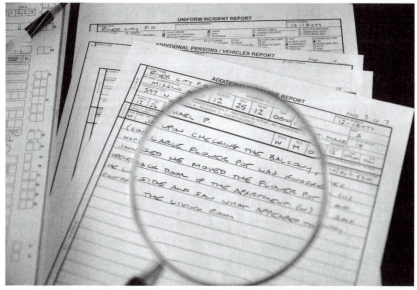

Handwritten reports, though not as common as they once were, still must be neatly written.

YOU CAN'T READ WHAT YOU CAN'T SEE

Let's talk about a couple of visual issues. Neatness is a good place to start. If you're writing reports by hand[2] for some reason, you must write neatly. That means print unless your cursive is exceedingly neat. Personally, I don't know anyone whose cursive is neat enough to use in a police report, so if you're thinking about it, you might want to think again.

If even your printing is horrible (you know who you are!), use block letters. If the reader picks up your report and it looks to him like it was written in Egyptian hieroglyphics or some kind of ancient cuneiform, it certainly won't be very clear to him. Use black ink, too.[3] That's the professional business standard.

---

2 Probably not as common an event as when I came on the job, but even in today's computerized world, you may find yourself writing the occasional report by hand.

3 Unless your department dictates otherwise. A few require blue ink so that the original document can be more easily determined.

But handwriting reports is going out of style, isn't it? No question. For the sake of neatness alone, it is best to type reports. This pretty quickly does away with the penmanship problem. Of course, as is the case in life, this solution brings up a couple other issues.

Size of the print is one issue. Make sure you use a large enough point size. Twelve or fourteen is usually best. This ensures that someone can read it without squinting.

Likewise, use a common font. Arial,[4] Times New Roman, and Courier are some of the most common ones and a sure bet. But I'd say that any font that is clear and legible is acceptable. You may find one you prefer (I'm partial to Garamond, Book Antiqua, and Bookman Old Style), and that's alright—unless your favorite font is Olde English Script or something else that is barely legible. And save the Star Trek Klingon font for the fan-boy newsletters, not your police reports.

Some agencies specify report font and format. Some utilize report-writing programs that force a particular font or limit choices. If your agency does, here's a good plan: follow that format! Always remember who signs your paycheck.

Regarding format, if the agency doesn't require a specific format, a good general rule is to *single*-space your text but *double*-space between paragraphs.

The human eye is used to reading single-spaced writing. This is what you see in books, newspapers, and magazines. You're probably reading this text right now in single-space format. It's quite common. Most people will have no difficulty reading this format.

I recommend the double space between paragraphs in order to visually break up the page. This is easier on the eye. The visual element is important. A reader sees a page-length single block of print as discouraging. A broken-up page is more inviting. It also makes it easier for the reader to find his place if he stops and starts again or to find a particular location within the report. It could be you rereading the report in court, trying to find a quote or the point at which you read Miranda rights to the suspect. Or it might be the detective reviewing the report for his investigation, looking for particular probable cause elements or a lead that he intends to follow up on.

---

4   I despise Arial. Arial sucks. But I have to concede that it is a common font and that, for some reason, a fair number of people like it. Doug does.

In any event, the double space between paragraphs makes for a more visually appealing report that is easier to refer back to. Over the course of an entire report, all it costs you is a few extra taps on the **ENTER** key.

Another rule of typing is DON'T WRITE IN ALL CAPS! In today's Internet age, writing in all caps is considered shouting. No one likes to be shouted at. ISN'T THAT RIGHT?

Even though the police report isn't necessarily being written for online reading,[5] most readers today have that background. Even the least computer literate of people today exchange e-mails and are aware of the online protocol regarding shouting (and those crutches we know as "emoticons").

An interesting sidenote here that we'll discuss when we get to slang. I've noticed some shortened version of informal, Internet English creeping into police reports within the last year or two. Although I agree with observing certain protocols such as not typing in all caps, I'm not about to support making it acceptable to write, `"The susp. jetted 2 the store 2nite."` But we'll get into that a little later.

A second reason not to write in all caps is once again visual. Writing in all capital letters creates a homogeneous look that is unfamiliar to the human eye and difficult to read. If you choose not to double-space between paragraphs, this effect is heightened.

I've heard some officers complain that it is just *so* much easier to click on the Caps Lock key and go to town on the report. Just type away. Don't have to worry about capitalization or anything. I have one word for that.

Lame.

Here's another word for it.

Weak.

Want to go for the hat trick? OK, here it is.

Lazy.

It takes very little practice to learn to type. Most people are able to type today as a matter of necessity. Part of learning to type is learning

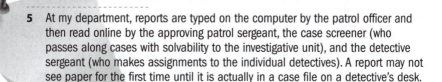

5   At my department, reports are typed on the computer by the patrol officer and then read online by the approving patrol sergeant, the case screener (who passes along cases with solvability to the investigative unit), and the detective sergeant (who makes assignments to the individual detectives). A report may not see paper for the first time until it is actually in a case file on a detective's desk.

to use the shift key and to properly capitalize. Put in the small time investment to learn this necessary skill. The miniscule amount of time and effort you're saving by hitting Caps Lock and then just typing along do not even come close to outweighing the visual clarity you give up. Every reader down the road will thank you for it.

The reality of today's world is that you need to learn to type. You won't be functional in this profession if you can't type.

Lastly, some word processor spell-check features will not function on words in all caps. The program simply assumes the word is an acronym. That would explain why I received a report one night on patrol with phrases like

THE ARGUEMENT CONTINUED IN THE LIVIVNGROON

and

HE HERD HER CALL THE VICTIM, "A FUMB BITHCH, AND FUCKING STUPIN"

and

HE SAW HIM PUCH HER TOW TIMES IN THECHEST AREA, CUASING REDNESS ON HER LEFT BREST.

Because that looks so horrible in all caps, here's a look at it properly capitalized but still with the errors:

The arguement continued in the livivngroon

and

He herd her call the victim, "a fumb bithch, and fucking stupin"

and

He saw him puch her tow times in thechest area, cuasing redness on her left brest.

Sure, some good proofreading would have caught those errors. But if the report had been properly capitalized, a spell-check function would have pointed them out, too. But neither event occurred, and this report came through to me as a supervisor. The thing is, the officer who wrote it is a crackerjack troop. He's a SWAT team member and a Defensive Tactics Instructor. He had several years on the job at the time of the report. He was and is anything but lazy or incompetent.

He also uses proper capitalization today.

In the end, you want your report to be something a person wants to read. You don't want it to be something that causes the reader to squint, groan, rub his eyes, or curse your name in perpetuity. So write with clear text and in a clear format.

IN ORDER TO WRITE, WRITE IN ORDER

Write your report in chronological order. *Chronological order* means in time order. Because you are writing this report, the order being referred to is *your* chronological order. A police report doesn't begin **"Once upon a time"** with the participants' experience but, rather, with the police officer's experience. In other words, I'm talking about the order in which you experienced the events. This is a technical report and you are the reporter. Therefore, the chronology of this report will center on *you* as the touchstone.

It may be necessary during your report to reflect someone else's account of events. The reporting of these events happens within the confines of your report. These accounts should also be reported chronologically but within the larger chronology of your report.

Confusing? It can be at first, until you get the hang of it. But it isn't nearly so confusing as trying to read a report with a messed up chronology.

Think of the report as a movie.

Reports should be written in chronological order.

Photo courtesy of M. J. Rose Images.

But *not* a Quentin Tarantino[6] movie.

You are the narrator of this movie. Heck, you . . . are . . . the . . . *star!*

Your report will usually begin in one of two ways. You will be dispatched to a call or you'll come upon some sort of situation yourself. In any event, you need to set the scene for the reader. Start simply with

> **On DATE at TIME hours, I (Officer Strosahl)**
> **was dispatched to 234 Melody Lane on a report**
> **of a burglary.**

What does this accomplish? Well, in one sentence, you've established when these events occur, who you are, and where your little adventure is beginning. This puts the reader squarely into the scene. It is clear who you are, what you're up to, and when you're doing it.

You might also include here any information that the dispatcher provides you with prior to arriving on the call—if, say, there was a possibility that the burglar was still in the house or that the victim suspected someone in particular. In a case such as a domestic dispute, what the reporting party told the 911 operator can be extraordinarily important for a variety of reasons. The issue of what you knew and when you knew it may come up at a later date.

Once you've established the date and time and set the table with your introductory statement, continue your report in chronological order. Remember, this is in time order. Whose time order? Yours. Write about the events in the order that you experienced them.

So, after being dispatched or making the decision to engage in self-initiated activity, what came next? What happened when you arrived? What did you observe about the location that was relevant? Was the weather relevant? Was it light or dark outside? What was the artificial lighting like? Could any of these things matter?

Sure. All of them could matter considerably. Or none of them could matter at all. If the fact is relevant, include it. We'll discuss that in the chapter on the COMPLETE pillar.

---

6 Tarantino wrote and directed such films as *Pulp Fiction* and *Reservoir Dogs*. In both films, he tells the story by going back and forth throughout the time line of events. He carries off the technique masterfully—the films are gripping. However, such a technique would be a confusing proposition in a police report.

Once on scene, whom did you talk to? What did you observe about that person? Was that person excited? Nervous? Angry? Intoxicated? Bleeding or otherwise injured?[7]

What did that person say?

What actions did you take? Record all of them, even if the outcome of the action was a big nothing. Exhausting options is sometimes a necessity in police work, and if you did it, you need to capture it in the report.

Once your investigation is complete, make sure to close your report with a disposition of some kind. Let readers know you really did mean to be finished with this report. Don't leave them hanging or wondering. That's like the episode of the old sitcom *M*A*S*H* in which the troops all read a murder mystery only to find the final page missing. Everyone went crazy wondering who did it and arguing about it. (They never did find out, because the aged writer couldn't recall the details of that particular novel when they telephoned her).

Or, if you're looking for a more contemporary example, anyone remember the episode of *The Office* when they found the screenplay written by Michael, the boss? The workers sat around the conference room while he was out and read lines in character from the script until they got to the end. Or at least, they thought it was the end because it just stopped. There was no resolution or indication that the script was over, other than the hero having parachuted from a plane.

How can you avoid a "Michael cliffhanger"?

Let the reader know how you wrapped things up. Did you give the victim the report number and some contact information? Was the case referred to detectives for further investigation? Did you put evidence on the property book? Did you make an arrest and book someone into jail?

How did this little movie, starring you, end?

And did you get the girl?

Oops. Wrong movie.

Incidentally, if you're the kind of person who also likes to use emoticons, you could always type the words NOTHING FOLLOWS at the end of your report. It's kind of an Army thing to do, but it works.[8]

---

7   On graveyard patrol, expect all five, especially the fourth—intoxication.

8   A lot of Army stuff works, as I discovered during my enlistment. It's just that a lot also doesn't.

THAT'S WHAT THEY SAY

When you interview someone and that person gives you a statement, include that statement within the larger framework of your chronology/ time line:

> `I spoke to Jackson, who told me the following`
> `regarding his burglary:`

Then start a new paragraph with a paraphrase of Jackson's statement. When his statement is completed, somehow let the reader know that you are returning to your own narrative. For example,

> `After taking Jackson's statement, I examined`
> `the point of entry.`

What is *paraphrasing*? It is relating what someone else has told you in your own words and in general terms. It isn't an exact quote, but the meaning is not changed. The purpose is to pare down an entire conversation into a succinct summary. You then present that summary in your report to the reader, who thankfully does not have to weed through the sometimes painful process of interviewing a drunken idiot at zero dark thirty in the morning.

Most of your report with regard to victim statements will be a paraphrase. Here's a portion of a burglary report with an example of the use of paraphrase:

> *On DATE at TIME hours, I (Officer Strosahl) was dispatched to 234 Malarkey Lane on a report of a burglary. Upon arrival, I contacted the victim, Tom Jackson. Jackson told me the following:*

> `He left for work at approximately 0730 hours`
> `this morning. When he returned at 2215 hours,`
> `he discovered his front door standing open. He`
> `went inside, but no one was there. However,`
> `his large screen television was missing.`

> *I asked Jackson if he knew who might have done this.*

> `He did not.`

> *After speaking with Jackson, I examined the front door, which appeared to be the point of entry. I noted tool marks on the door jamb consistent with a pry tool.*

The shaded section represents what Jackson told the officer. However, the officer isn't reporting Jackson's exact words or the specific flow of the questions and answers that garnered this information. He merely reports that he requested the information and then accurately[9] summarizes the response.

Why not just quote the guy? Wouldn't that be more accurate?

Sure. And if you want to tape record and then transcribe every interview you ever conduct, be my guest.

I once knew an officer who would write in his reports: **I contacted [suspect, witness or victim] and he told me the following:** whereupon he would write several long paragraphs of this person's statement in quotation marks.[10] Sometimes these "quotations" would go on for a page or more.[11]

I take no issue with this format if you *paraphrase* your interviewee. That's exactly what I did in the previous example. But unless you have an absolutely amazing memory, I heartily doubt that you can quote someone *exactly* for half a page or longer. And if you have a memory that good, what are you doing in law enforcement? Go to Vegas or something. Use that skill to get rich. Retire to an island somewhere where it never rains.

The point is, quoting someone like that just isn't practical. What's more, it isn't efficient. It also makes for one drawn out, boring report. The reader doesn't need to see the Q and A. The reader needs to know the relevant information. So you paraphrase.

But what about quoting? Should you ever quote someone?

Of course you should.

But when?

Simple. Quote whenever appropriate.

---

9 One of the pillars we'll discuss in more detail in a later chapter.

10 The funny part about it, too, was that even though he was quoting the person, he referred to him in the third person instead of the first. If you don't know why that's funny, come back to this section after you read the grammar section, and then you will. Trust me.

11 I was a sergeant at the time. He wasn't one of my officers, so I didn't get his reports too often. When I did, I told him not to do this and explained why. But instead of taking an actual lesson, he just made sure I didn't get his reports to review anymore. He was kind of a meatball, anyway. Don't be a meatball.

Paraphrase a witness's statement, but quote him when appropriate.

I imagine you just rolled your eyes or maybe even threw this book against the wall with a pronounced scream of "Smart alec!" All I know is that I ducked as I typed the words, just in case.

But honestly, my friend, that is the best answer I can give. Law enforcement is a field that requires considerable judgment and common sense. People who are lacking in those qualities struggle mightily. This holds true with police reports, too. You have to be the judge of when it is appropriate to quote someone in your report.

I'll help you a bit, though.

A quote should have purpose. It should illuminate an important point or facet in the investigation. Therefore, I'd recommend quoting someone any time that the particular words he used stood out to you for some reason. Perhaps those exact words painted a vivid picture of his frame of mind. Or they described what he saw or did more accurately than any paraphrase could.

Try this:

> I asked Thompson to describe the injury he saw. Thompson told me, "His hand looked like it'd been through a meat grinder."

Paints a picture, doesn't it?

Another reason for a direct quote would be if he made an admission of some kind. Compare the two following passages involving a homicide case:

> 1. Rogers told me that he encountered the victim in the parking lot, where he'd been waiting for the victim and planning to assault him. The two argued over money that the victim owed Rogers. Rogers became angry, drew his pistol and shot the victim in the head.
>
> 2. Rogers told me that he encountered the victim in the parking lot, where he'd been waiting to "waylay his ass" and "bust a cap in his no-paying, worthless hide." The two argued over money that the victim owed Rogers. Rogers said that he "got really pissed" and drew his pistol. He pointed the gun at the victim and "blew that bitch into next week."

Which paragraph is more powerful? How do the quotations affect the paragraph?

As you can see, the reader gets a flavor of Rogers, his state of mind, and his intent due to the use of quotes. Though the flavor and tone of Rogers are good to have, his state of mind and his intent are important for legal reasons. By his own admission, Rogers waited in the parking lot with the sole intent of confronting the victim and probably shooting him. If this becomes a murder charge (a pretty likely result, given the head shot), does Rogers' statement indicate premeditation? And is premeditation an important element in a murder charge?

Yep, and Yep.

The other thing to consider about this paragraph and using these quotations is that these same words will come back to haunt the suspect later in an interview or at trial. It is extremely difficult for someone to deny his own exact words. It's much easier to deny a general sentiment.

For instance, following is a pair of hypothetical transcripts from a post-incident interview by a detective in our Rogers murder case. The first transcript exists in a world in which the officer initially wrote report example number one, the second with report example number two—the one with the quotes.

Question: Mr. Rogers, what did you intend to do when Mr. McFeeley arrived in the parking lot?

Answer: I don't know. Talk to him, I guess.

Q: About what?

A: The money he owed me. He needed to pay me. I gotta get paid.

Q: What if he didn't or couldn't pay you?

A: I'd be mad.

Q: Would you hurt him?

A: Maybe, just a little.

Q: How?

A: Just shove him some, I suppose.

Q: So you didn't plan to use the gun?

A: Hell, no! That's just for protection, nothing else.

Q: So what did you mean when you told the officer you planned to assault Mr. McFeeley?

A: Just like I said. I might smack him or twist his arm a little. But I didn't plan on doing no shooting.

At this point, has the detective essentially lost the element of premeditation in this case? Pretty much, he has. It's not a done deal, but the row just became a lot harder to hoe. Contrast it with the following, in which the detective has the ammunition of the suspect's own words from the officer's police report:

Question: Mr. Rogers, what did you intend to do when Mr. McFeeley arrived in the parking lot?

Answer: I don't know. Talk to him, I guess.

Q: About what?

A: The money he owed me. He needed to pay me. I gotta get paid.

Q: What if he didn't or couldn't pay you?

A: I'd be mad.

Q: Would you hurt him?

A: Maybe, just a little.

Q: How?

A: Just shove him some, I suppose.

Q: So you didn't plan to use the gun?

A: Hell, no! That's just for protection, nothing else.

Q: So what did you mean when you told the officer you planned to "bust a cap in his no-paying, worthless hide" if Mr. McFeeley didn't pay you the money?

A: I, uh...

Q: What does "bust a cap" mean?

A: It means, uh, to shoot someone.

Q: With a gun?

A: Yeah.

Q: Like the one you had?

A: Well, like any gun, I guess.

Q: But like the one you had, too?

A: Sure.

Q: So when you came to the parking lot and waited for McFeeley, you were planning to "waylay his ass"?

A: Well...

Q: Is that what you told the officer?

A: Yeah. I was planning to talk to the guy.

Q: And if he didn't pay?

A: I'd do what I had to do.

Q: Did that include "busting a cap"?

A: Yeah, I guess it did.

> **Q: So you planned to shoot him if he didn't pay?**
> **A: Yeah. Bitch owed me money.**

Ladies and gentlemen, we now have premeditation—first degree murder (or whatever the equivalent is in your jurisdiction).

Now, am I saying that every murder investigation hinges on the reporting officer selecting the correct quotations? Of course not. Most detectives can find a dozen or more ways to get to the truth—most times. But sometimes, a case may only present one or two avenues. And interviewing and interrogating are as much an art as a science. One key to a successful interrogation is having a lever. A telling quote can be a mighty powerful lever.

Hate crimes are another example of a type of report in which a quote might be critical. Let's say a suspect assaulted a black male with a baseball bat. His motivation appeared to be simply because of the victim's race. Which of the following tells a better story?

1. *Paraphrase without quote.* **The suspect told me that he waited until the victim had turned his back and then struck him with the baseball bat in the head. He described the victim with a racial epithet.**

2. *Quote.* **The suspect told me that he "waited 'til that nigger turned his ugly ass around and then I cold-cocked him upside the head with my Louisville Slugger."**

Which is clearer? Which conveys the state of mind and precise hatred of the suspect? For that matter, compare the relative impact upon the judge and jury hearing this case.[12] Granted, one is profane and shocking,[13] but the issue here is clarity. We'll discuss the issue of accuracy later.

12 With a quote like this, I'd lay odds a smart defense attorney pleads his client out as quickly as possible and avoids the courtroom like the plague.

13 As I've alluded to before, anyone not expecting to encounter the profane and the shocking in the criminal justice field should readjust his or her expectations—or career plans. Although it is a professional field, criminal justice deals frequently with the dark side of human nature.

Hopefully, you now have a handle on when it might be appropriate to quote someone, be it a suspect, victim, or witness. Aside from those quotes, you will paraphrase statements within the framework of your report.

One last word on paraphrasing (for a little while at least). Try to avoid the "I asked, he said" mantra. This pitfall, in reality, is barely paraphrasing someone. It goes something like this:

```
I asked Jackson what time he left for work.
He said he left at seven-thirty that morning.
I asked when he returned home. He said it
was about 2215 hours. I asked him what he saw
when he arrived home. He said he saw that his
door was standing open. I asked if it looked
like it had been kicked or what? He said it
appeared to have been pried open with a crow-
bar or something. I asked if there was anyone
inside when he arrived. He said there was
not. I asked him if anything was missing. He
said yes. I asked him what was missing and
he said his big screen TV was gone. I asked
Jackson if he had any idea who might have
broken into his house. He said he didn't know
who it could be.
```

Now let's read our earlier version of that section of the Jackson burglary report again, this time avoiding the "I asked, he said" mantra.

```
Jackson stated that he left for work at ap-
proximately 0730 hours this morning. When he
returned at 2215 hours, he discovered his
front door standing open. He went inside,
but no one was there. However, his large
screen television was missing.

I asked Jackson if he knew who might have
done this. He did not.
```

Which is an easier read? Which is clearer—not to mention more *concise* (meaning short or succinct, a feature we'll examine in a later chapter)? Let's look at the scoreboard for our answer. Example one is 140 words long. Example two? Fifty-five. Pretty simple math, huh?

The "I asked, he said" mantra is easy to fall into while writing the report. Experienced officers do it all the time. Sometimes you'll only notice it when you do a proofreading before turning in the report. Hopefully, you will be at the computer when you do this. In that case, you can do a little spot editing and tighten that paragraph considerably.

Always be crystal clear as to which statements belong to which party. Use attributions wherever necessary, such as "he said" or "Jackson said." Generally speaking, though, if you're paraphrasing someone for an extended period (say, a paragraph or more), you don't have to use those attributions on every line. For example, you'll notice in the preceding paragraph that every line doesn't contain a "Jackson said" or "he said" in it. Yet, as you read it, it is clear that this is Jackson's statement: **Jackson stated that he left for work at approximately 0730 hours this morning.** This—coupled with the end of that passage in which the reporting officer clearly states he is asking a question and Jackson answers it—creates a bookend effect. This technique allows you to avoid the "I asked, he said" mantra, as well as the "he said, he said" chant.

Never attribute a quote to more than one person. Unless they speak in stereo, in cadence, or maybe spontaneously burst into song, people generally don't use the same exact words as each other. So as a general rule, don't even paraphrase a group. For example,

No/Never: **I interviewed Foxy, Loxy, and Moxie, who all three said that Loosey Goosey was as "crazy as a rooster!"**

Better (but not great): **I interviewed Foxy, Loxy, and Moxie. All three told me that they felt Loosey Goosey was mentally unstable.**

Best: **I interviewed Foxy, Loxy, and Moxie. Loxy said that Loosey Goosey was as "crazy as a rooster!" Foxy and Moxie both agreed with this sentiment.**

Of course, an actual report would contain considerably more detail. Ideally, you would have three separate statements by Foxy, Loxy, and Moxie. A juicy quote from each wouldn't hurt, either.

"DE PLANE"[14] LANGUAGE

If you want to be CLEAR in your report writing, it is best to write in plain language.

In the old days, back when cops carried Sam Colts and rode horseback, police reports were purposefully written in what I'm sure was intended to be a professional manner but was really just not very clear [hmmm—sort of like that last sentence]. What I mean is that they said and did a lot of things that might have made their reports sound more like police reports but did not necessarily make them clear. Clear? Well, let's forge ahead and you'll see what I mean.

One way to keep things clear is to not abbreviate. Write out your words. Sure, I suppose words like *etc.* for *et cetera* or even *approx.* for *approximately* are all right. However, I've seen some reports that were just replete with abbreviations and acronyms. It's confusing, even to someone who is familiar with them. It's time-consuming and actually tiring, too, because you have to do the work in your head of translating the abbreviation or acronym into an actual word or phrase.

You may find that you have the need to use an abbreviation, however. For instance, if you intend to use the phrase "ACCOUNTABILITY IN MANAGEMENT" repeatedly in your report, it only makes sense to abbreviate it at some point. How do you make sure that abbreviation is clear to the reader, though?

Here's where I have to agree with the Army way. Write out the word the first time, followed by the abbreviation in parentheses. Then use the abbreviation for the remainder of the report. For example,

    The police department will utilize the Ac-
    countability in Management (AIM) system to
    measure output and outcome. All divisions
    will present information in the prescribed
    AIM format at weekly AIM meetings. A yearly
    AIM report will be issued.

---

14 Anyone remember *Fantasy Island?* Come on. Anyone?

Now the reader knows what the acronym AIM means. You can use it a hundred more times if you need to and the meaning will be clear.

Besides abbreviation, other enemies of clarity are jargon and slang. These are similar terms. *Jargon* is specialized language that usually surrounds a particular profession or activity. Law enforcement has its own jargon. So does firefighting, the military, and most sports. Jargon is a kind of technical term that most people outside of that circle would not understand.

Any hockey fans in the crowd? If you are, you might understand the following transcript from a radio broadcast of a Philadelphia Flyers game.[15] If not, you may be lost.

> **"Giroux takes the breakout pass from Pronger. He carries across the red line with speed. He splits the 'D' and is in on a breakaway. The goaltender cuts down the angle. Giroux dekes. He goes to his backhand and puts it upstairs. Goal! Top shelf, where mama keeps the jam! And that's the hat trick for number 28!"**

OK, so you non–hockey fans out there, did that make sense? Now, don't whine—there was nothing in there about offsides or icing or any of the other supposedly confusing rules in hockey. And I know you know something good happened, right? But what, exactly?

That's the point about jargon. A hockey player or fan would easily understand that description. It would paint a vivid picture in his mind. But to the uninitiated, it's unclear. Why? Because it is full of jargon.

Moving on to law enforcement jargon—what's that? You want to know what the hockey broadcast meant? OK. Twist my arm. Here it is. Just so that you aren't losing sleep about it.[16]

15 Flyers rule. I totally made this little broadcast up for the purposes of showing slang, but I'm reasonably certain something very similar to it gets broadcast every day of the season.

16 And so you can see how different plain speech is from jargon. Keep in mind, though, that jargon can sometimes speed up *verbal* communication among people in the know. It's not *verboten*. It just doesn't go in a police report.

`Giroux takes the breakout pass from Pronger.` *Pronger passed Giroux the puck from inside the defensive zone— that's their own end of the ice.* `He carries across the red line with speed.` *Giroux skates quickly across the red line that is at center ice, controlling the puck with his stick.* `He splits the "D" and is in on a breakaway.` *Using his speed, he manages to skate between the two defensemen. Because of that, there is no one left between him and the goaltender—this is called a breakaway. He still has the puck.* `The goaltender cuts down the angle.` *The goalie skates toward Giroux to give him less open net to shoot at.* `Giroux dekes.` *He handles the puck with his stick quickly, faking the goaltender.* `He goes to his backhand and puts it upstairs.` *He uses the back of his stick blade to shoot the puck instead of the forehand. He shoots high.* `Goal!` *The puck goes into the net, scoring a goal.* `Top shelf, where mama keeps the jam!` *"Top shelf" is slang for the upper portion of the net. The thing about the jam is just a great sports saying.* `And that's the hat trick for number 28!` *A hat trick is three goals in a game by the same player. Giroux wears the number 28 on his jersey.*

Make more sense now? Great. Get with me later and I'll explain icing, too.

OK, moving on to law enforcement jargon—for real this time. An example might be a common law enforcement term: *collar,* which means *to arrest;* or *perp* for *perpetrator.*[17] Another is *deuce* for a *DUI* (driving under the influence). Even though these are common jargon terms used in many parts of the country in the law enforcement field, it would not be considered CLEAR to write in a report

`I collared the suspect for a deuce.`

Even though most every cop would understand you, most civilians (or even others within the criminal justice field) would not. Instead, you should write

`I arrested the suspect for DUI.`

---

17 Does anyone still say "perp," though? That brings up another problem that is more common with slang than jargon—how contemporary is the term?

This is a technical law enforcement report, however. Therefore, it is all right to use general police terms, such as *suspect* or *DUI,* or something like, **"I contacted the subject at the convenience store."** This is a very mild use of police jargon. Why so? Well, do you talk that way in your private life? Does anyone actually say, **"Hey honey, I was down at the store earlier and I contacted a subject"**? If you do, you're spending way too much time at work. No, most people would say, **"I was down at the store and I bumped into a guy I know"** or something along those lines. So *contacted* and *subject* are actually a mild form of jargon.

Sometimes officers use phrases in an effort to sound official or detached. These phrases get used because they sound like something you'd read in an official police report. You want an example? OK, here's one: **The window was small in size.** Think about that one for a second. What else would it be small in? Color? Scent?

Or another: **They had a verbal argument.** What other kind of argument might they have? A telepathic one? Oh, I suppose that they could be having a *legal* argument, but that probably wouldn't be a clear word choice, would it? *Dispute* would be a better word for that. No, we're talking here about an argument. Of course it's verbal. Rather than wasting space on the word *verbal,* it might be better to describe the argument. For instance, the argument may have been "heated" or "constrained." This gives the reader a picture of what the argument was like, so it serves a purpose.

The point is this: although used in an effort to sound more official and coplike, these phrases actually muddy the waters. They are redundant and less than clear. Avoid them. Speak plainly.

Having said all of that, certain police terminology in reports is OK to use. Phrases like **"I double-locked the handcuffs"** or **"I patted him down for weapons"** are rather specific to law enforcement (and therefore a form of jargon) but perfectly acceptable. Generally speaking, your primary audience for the report is people associated with law enforcement. They should be familiar with these terms, so the report should be clear to them. That is why we're discussing jargon—to make sure our reports aren't unclear due to the use of jargon. If you do use police terms, just don't get too obscure or get into a lot of abbreviations (remember what we said about those?) or acronyms.

Slang is essentially social jargon. It may be particular to a region, culture, age-group, or belief system, among other things. Slang may refer to nouns, such as calling a vehicle "a ride" or "a whip" or calling an apartment "a crib." It may refer to verbs, as in **"He was sitting around, just chillin'"** or **"He was bookin' down the street."** Slang pops up frequently as an adjective, such as **"That was a *sick* concert"** (meaning *good, fun, exciting*). It might also derive from a particular medium, such as the Internet. Thus, slang includes Internet-speak like, **"I went 2 the store 2nite b4 dinner."**

Like jargon, slang causes issues of clarity. More than that, slang is unprofessional. It is unclear because the word or phrase might mean something different in one part of the country than another, or among one social group or another. It is unprofessional because it simply is. It is a low, informal use of the English language.

For comparison's sake, take German, for example. For a country roughly the size of Oregon, there are a surprising number of different variations or regional dialects of the German language within the borders of Germany. Some are considerably different from others. However, there is what is known as *hochdeutsch* or "high German," which is the basic foundation of the language that everyone agrees on. That is the version that is taught in school. It is the version that business is conducted in and in which legal affairs are resolved.

Does English have an equivalent of *hochdeutsch*? Not so much. "Proper" English is about as close as it comes. So, in order to be professional and CLEAR, use proper English. *Verstehen Sie mich?*[18]

Another danger of slang, aside from being unclear and unprofessional, is that it is usually short-lived. Five years after the fact, the meaning of the word may not be as clear, as it may not be used in the same fashion any longer. It may even mean something else. For example, I had just managed to figure out the right way to use the word *whack* in a way that didn't mean something similar to *hit* or *smack* about the time that particular usage of the word went out of style.

Does the word *groovy* ring a bell with anyone?

---

18 Hey, if I lived in Germany for almost three years and couldn't learn the phrase for "Do you understand me?" I'd be pretty much lost, don't ya think? After "Where is the bathroom?" and "Give me a beer, please," I think that "Do you understand me?" ranks pretty high on the scale of phrases I need to know.

Of course, *cool* seems to have enjoyed a steady following for decades now. Using *cool* in a report would probably not cause an issue regarding clarity. But it's still slang, so don't use it, simply on professional grounds.

In addition to avoiding slang, you should not use derogatory terms of any kind. This includes terms that refer in a derogatory fashion to race, gender, or sexual terms. Likewise, profanity has no place in a police report. None of these are professional, and many denote a bias that a professional law enforcement officer simply should not have.

Every rule has an exception. The exception to the use of jargon, slang, and derogatory terms is, of course, when quoting someone. If you are quoting an individual, quote him *exactly*. This is true despite his use of poor grammar, profanity, epithets, or jargon. The purpose of a quote is to illuminate exactly what a person said because it is relevant to the situation in the report.

OOPS!

Everyone makes mistakes. You're bound to make a few when writing your police report. If that happens, hopefully you are typing the report on your computer. Most keyboards have a secret magic button that I'm about to share with you. Don't tell anyone.

This button allows you to erase your mistakes so that you can type the correct word in its place. Crazy cool, huh?

The key looks like this: ← **BACKSPACE.**

That's the great thing about typing reports. Inst-o, prest-o, fix-o.

Anyway, we'll get to spell-checking, grammar-checking, and proofreading later. For now, just about all you need to know about fixing a mistake when you're typing is that one, wonderful key I just told you about.

Photo courtesy of M. J. Rose Images.

The magic fix-it key for report writers.

So what if you are trapped somewhere and have to handwrite a report? No problem. Heck, in the old days, we wrote them all. And we never made mistakes, either. We were too busy walking to work in the snow with no shoes. Seven miles, my friend. Uphill. Both ways. We didn't have time for mistakes.

OK, so maybe we made a few. And when we did, out came the Wite-Out. If you need to use Wite-Out to correct a report, use the stuff judiciously. That means don't use it frequently and don't use a ton of it when you do apply some. If the report you're turning in looks like a junior high topographical map assignment for geology class or something—yeah, that's probably too much.

If you are handwriting a report and make a mistake, and you have no Wite-Out, what should you do? As an absolute last resort, you may strike through the error with a single line and initial above the strike-through. This should be used only as a last resort, when you don't have Wite-Out and don't have time to rewrite the report.

I say this in the basic law enforcement academy, too, but whenever I'd get the first batch of reports turned in, it never failed that at least three or four would be riddled with strike-throughs and initials. I'd point this out to the offending students, and then came the excuses: "But you said we could...blah, blah, blah."

Want to make things easy for everyone? Type your reports if at all possible.

NAMES, NUMBERS, AND TIME

How do you make sure your report is clear when it comes to names, numbers and time?

Names are the trickiest of the three, so let's tackle that first. The best approach to names is to use a person's last name whenever possible. Not only is it the most clear, but this also provides a little bit of clinical distance in the report, lending it an air of objectivity. However, it is also a good idea to use the person's full name the first time he is mentioned. For example,

I spoke to Adam Deadmarsh about his concussion.

On subsequent uses, you refer to the subject only by his last name. For example,

Deadmarsh said it was getting better.

That works wonderfully, if you only have one Deadmarsh in the report. What if you are at a domestic dispute? There may be several people there with the same last name. In this case, we will sacrifice a little bit of that clinical distance in the greater interest of clarity. In other words, use people's first names. For example,

> `I also spoke to Adam's brother, Tim. Tim told`
> `me that he saw the entire incident.`

In the interests of clarity, don't do what I have seen some officers succumb to in their reports, that is, to use the first initial and last name of each subject. This is terribly confusing, particularly once you get above two people. For example,

> `While I interviewed A. Deadmarsh and T. Dead-`
> `marsh, L. Deadmarsh waited out on the front`
> `porch. At the same time, Officer Strosahl`
> `interviewed S. Deadmarsh in the kitchen.`

Contrast that with

> `While I interviewed Adam and Tim, Larry`
> `waited out on the front porch. At the same`
> `time, Officer Strosahl interviewed Susan in`
> `the kitchen.`

Which of these two passages is the clearest? It seems obvious, but I have pointed this out to several officers throughout the years. It always surprises them when they realize how unclear it really is to use those initials and last name instead of a first name, particularly to someone who was not present at the call.

That's one thing to remember regarding clarity in general. Something may seem clear to you because you were on the call, at the scene, and involved in the situation. Most of the people reading your report were not. So anything you can do to make the report as clear as possible is helpful. Not only that, but always try to see your report through the filter of "Would this make sense to someone who wasn't there?"

The last thing I'll say about names here is that you have to be consistent. If you start calling a subject in your report "Deadmarsh," then call him that for the entire report. Don't start calling him "Adam" midway through the report, then revert back to "Deadmarsh" at some point later in the report. This is extraordinarily confusing. You'll probably have the sergeant calling you into the office to say, "Look, I don't understand why you arrested this Adam guy. As far as I can tell, your probable cause is for this Deadmarsh fellow!"

In our adult lives, we relate to people differently than we did when we were growing up by how we address them. Teachers always wanted to be called "Mr." or "Mrs." as a sign of respect (except for the cool ones who asked to be called by their first names). Coaches called us by our last names to help show dominance or to create the illusion of superiority over us. We call our supervisors at work "Sergeant" or "Lieutenant" or by the more informal "Sarge" or "El-Tee," depending on the circumstances. We typically call our friends by their first names, and we call our really close friends and lovers by nicknames. We know that changing what we call other people doesn't change who they are, but it does affect how we and others relate to them.

Because of this, we can use a name in a report to help gain sympathy or lack thereof toward a specific person. For example, you can help the detectives or prosecutors identify with a victim by consistently using the person's first name throughout a report while conversely using the suspect's last name to "depersonalize" him. It may sound simple and silly, but it really does work.

This is tricky business, because it isn't as objective as a police report maybe should be. So I'll leave you to examine the ethics of this type of phrasing on your own and decide for yourself if this is a tactic you wish to employ. On the one hand, we sheepdogs are the guardians of the flock and should advocate on their behalf when they've encountered wolves. On the other hand, we have a duty to be objective reporters. You'll have to find your own comfort zone on this one.

Numbers are a little easier than names. There are grammatical rules to follow with regard to numbers. If you don't know what they are, go look them up. What I'll tell you here is only for the sake of clarity. You can present numbers in your report in one of three ways.

1. There are the Arabic numerals: 8, 12, 68.

2. There are the written words: eight, twelve, sixty-eight.

3. And there is the method for the completists among us: eight (8), twelve (12), sixty-eight (68).

Which brings us to time of day. Time should always be reflected in military hours. This is standard within the law enforcement field. Why do we use military time? Because it is clearer than standard time. *7:00* isn't clear enough. Even *7:00 PM* isn't clear enough. But *1900 hours* is. There is no question what time that is. No ambiguity. It happened at 1900 hours. When? Uh, 1900 hours, just like I said.

But what if you're a civilian and you're confused by military time? Well, I have four words for you.

Too bad. Learn it.

The only time you should use standard time instead of military time is when you're quoting someone. If the victim said, **"I got home at exactly five-thirty,"** then that's how you write it. Of course, in the interests of clarity, you may want to specify in your own narrative that he meant 1730 hours.

SPELL IT, SPELL IT, SPELL IT OUT LOUD

Who's a good speller? Raise your hand. Come on, be proud.

I'm seeing about two hands tentatively going up out there. All the other good spellers are looking around nervously, wondering if they should confess. The poor spellers are glaring, but forget about them for a moment. If you are a good speller, get that hand up high. Seriously. It is no longer a sin to be smart or to be a geek. We all know by now that the kids we called "nerds" or "geeks" while growing up are the ones making the big bucks now!

All right, there are a few hands. Good, good. Don't be shy about having a skill. Good spelling only makes your life easier when it comes to report writing.

Now put down your little bragging hands.

Poor spellers? Let's see those hands.

Now, there you go. Yeah, baby! No one is afraid to admit to being a poor speller. Every time I ask this question in a classroom, a host of arms fly upward with vigor and pride. Why is that? I have no idea, but it seems to be that way every session.

You can't lean on the poor spellers too hard, though. Even past presidents of this great nation have been less-than-adequate spellers.[19] Andrew Jackson was the seventh president and was a general and a warrior before

---

19 No, not Dan Quayle. He was a *vice* president, wise guy.

he became a politician. On the subject of spelling, "Old Hickory" once observed, "It is a damn poor mind indeed which can't think of at least two ways to spell any word." And he served two terms, from 1829 to 1837.

It was a good thing for him that *VETO* is a pretty simple word to spell, I guess.

So why do we even care about spelling? If a U.S. president didn't put much value on correct spelling, why should we?

It all goes back to professionalism. If you turn in a report that is full of spelling errors, it isn't professional. And any chink in your professional armor will lead people to wonder what else you aren't professional about. The image you project is important. So is doing a professional job.

If you're a good speller, then you're in like Flynn. But what if you're a poor speller? What can you do to avoid spelling mistakes in your report?

For starters, ask people how to correctly spell their names. As our nation continues to become increasingly more multicultural, you will encounter names that you are less familiar with. So ask the question, "How do you spell that?"

"OK," you're probably thinking, "but only if it is a name I never heard of. Not if the person's name is common."

Really? Perhaps it sounds silly, but in today's day and age, even the so-called standard spellings for first and last names have many variations. Say you've got a guy named Kevin Smith reporting a stolen vehicle. Easy enough, right? Or is it Kevan Smyth? Or Kevyn Smythe? Or Keven Smi-ythe? Or Cachanga Serpaap (pronounced Ke-VIN SMITH)? [20]

I don't know. And neither do you until you ask how it is spelled.

We no longer live in a world in which people conform to society. More and more, they expect society to conform to them. This manifests itself in giving babies names. Anyone can give their newborns any names they like. Any adult can change his name to any name he likes. And believe me, even if he didn't pick the name out, it will be spelled any way he chooses.

So ask the question, "How do you spell that?" What's the worst that can happen? The person will just look at you like you're stupid. I'd rather get that look than the one that says, "How can you not know that *Kevin Smith* is spelled C-A-C-H-A-N-G-A S-E-R-P-A-A-P? Duh."

20 I totally made this up as I was writing this. If that's actually your name, then that makes us, like, brothers or something. See you at Thanksgiving.

The English language is a goofy amalgam of other, not-so-similar languages. Anything with both Latin and Germanic roots is going to have a few conflicts, right? Throw in some French influence and you've got a nice, confusing mix. Add to that the fact that American English has been developing separately from British English for a couple hundred years, with different influences from different cultures and experiences. I absolutely pity anyone who has to learn English as a second language. Really. I think there are maybe two or three harder languages to learn as a second language in the entire world.

One of the wonderful things we have in English is words that sound exactly alike but are spelled differently and have different meanings. For example, find what is wrong with each of the following sentences:

1. **Role the dice while I eat this dinner roll.**

   Role is a noun, not a verb. It means a part or a function, such as in "the actor auditioned for the *role* of the leading man." It should be the verb, meaning (because it is dice) to toss or throw. That spelling is *Roll*.

   But then, is the second *roll* correct? Yes, it is. A dinner *roll* is a type of bread. It is spelled and sounds the same as the verb *to roll*.

   Nope. That's not confusing at all.

2. **With a waive of his hand, he waved the age requirement.**

   Let's look at *waive* first. It is used here as a noun, meaning to motion with the hand, usually to get attention or signal something. It should be spelled *wave*. Sounds the same, though. *Waive* is actually a verb. It means to give up something or allow an exemption. It is frequently used in law enforcement like this: "He *waived* his right to an attorney."

   Obviously, then, the second word should be *waived* instead of *waved*. *Waved* is the past tense of *to wave*.

   Wave can also be a noun, as in an ocean *wave* or another attack *wave*.

3. **I'll mete you at the meet market where justice will be meated out.**

   Uh-oh. It's the hat trick. Three variations.

   The first one, *mete*, actually belongs in the third position. *To mete* is to give or deliver. Just like in the sentence, "justice will be *meted* out." So, instead of *mete* you, what should it be?

Meet, meaning to come together. That part of the sentences should read, "I'll *meet* you…."

Saved the easiest one for last. *Meet* market should obviously be *meat* market. *Meat* is flesh, usually in the context of food. This last sentence should actually read, "I'll meet you at the meat market where justice will be meted out." But if you read it out loud both ways, it sounds the same.

That's English for ya.

There are all kinds of other wonderful idiosyncrasies, rules (most of which have as many exceptions as adherents), and patterns in English spelling that drive people crazy. Watch out for the more common ones, like *accept/except* or *principal/principle* or the ubiquitous *there/their/they're.*

Ultimately, the only way to get better at spelling (and vocabulary) is to learn the words. In the meantime, get yourself a dictionary. Use the spell-check function of your word processor. Just don't rely too heavily on spell-check. As I'm typing this manuscript, none of my three example sentences merited a red underline from spell-check. That's because even though I used the wrong words, I spelled them correctly.

Spell-check is a great tool, but it isn't the end all, be all of your spelling needs. The best option is to learn to spell better—and proofread carefully.

Aftur awl, iff yew misabuse wurds ore spel thim rong inn yore repourt, ewe doan't luk vary profeshinal.

GRAMMAR SUCKS

Bet you didn't think you'd see that in a book on report writing. You probably expected to hear about how *important* grammar is and how *wonderful* grammar is and how we all must bow and pray at the altar of the grammar gods.

I haven't lied to you yet, so I'm not going to start now.

Grammar sucks.

Especially English grammar. Part of the problem is that it is based upon such a mishmash of different languages that none of the rules are consistently followed. English is probably one of the hardest languages to learn (Finnish and Hungarian have more difficult grammar, but I don't know if they're harder to learn or not).

So, yeah, grammar sucks. But as long as we're talking about what sucks, let's look at law enforcement for a second.

This guy loves grammar.

Standing in the rain or out in the cold on a perimeter for several hours sucks.

So does going to a scene where someone died a week ago and the hot summer sun has been baking through the window all week long.

So does getting spit at and called names by someone who later files a complaint about how rude you were.

So does... well, you get the idea.

Grammar is what it is. We've got to work with it in order to make our meaning clear. Poor grammar in a police report can change the meaning of a sentence. It can make the entire report difficult to follow, depending on the structure. Poor grammar may allow someone else to twist meaning or cast doubt[21] on what is written in your report.

So grit your teeth. Learn about grammar. Buy a grammar guide,[22] just like you picked up a dictionary. Get acquainted. Get better.

21 And what nefarious creatures might want to do that? Defense attorneys.

22 I prefer *The Grammar Bible* by Strumpf and Douglas, but that's just one of many.

I'll help a little. But don't think I'm going to enjoy it any more than you will.

In fact, I'm going to put it off just a few more moments by telling a little report-writing war story. Yeah, I know they aren't as cool as the "I arrested some guy that I had to chase six blocks and then he fought with me" war stories, but it's better than delving into grammar right away, isn't it? So don't whine, and listen up.

This chapter is about clarity in your report. Some officers say that they only need to write well enough to spark their memory. Then they can testify in court to clarify anything that isn't entirely clear in the report. This may be true in a few lucky instances, but it is a foolish attitude to have as your default setting.

CASE IN POINT

In 1995, I arrested someone for possession of methamphetamine. He'd been at his parents' house acting a little crazy earlier in the night, seeing people that were driving by in cars and supposedly threatening to kill him. I thought that I'd settled it by convincing him he was simply seeing sinister things in everyday events and then getting everyone to agree to go to bed. Unfortunately, a couple of hours later, he was back up and at it again. This time, his paranoia had developed into suicidal manifestations and he also threatened his father's safety. So I took him into custody on a mental health hold, intending to take him to the hospital for evaluation. I searched him before putting him in my patrol car. I found a knife and methamphetamine.

Because there was no guarantee that the hospital would hold him for more than a few hours, I chose to book him into jail with a mental health advisory. The mental health professionals could then visit him in jail and evaluate him there; plus, the corrections officers would take precautions with him on the suicidal issue.

I booked him, put the drugs onto property, and wrote the report.

I never heard about this case again until February 1998. That's three years later, for those of you following along at home. That winter night, I opened up my issue of *Law Enforcement Digest (LED)* just like I did every other month. The *LED* is a publication edited by the Washington State Attorney General's Office for the purpose of reviewing legal decisions that affect law enforcement. The AG's Office provided interpretations of this new "case law" and suggestions on how to best navigate the subsequent legal waters.

(continued)

CASE IN POINT (CONTINUED)

There on page 7 was *State v. Dempsey*. My arrest.

Much to my surprise, the case had already been tried and adjudicated. The defense had stipulated to the facts as represented in my report. This means that they all agreed that the facts in my report were true and accurate.[23]

The defense lawyer raised an issue challenging the legality of my search. He claimed it was pre-textual and so forth, but the trial judge overrode the objection without hearing testimony. The defendant was found guilty on summary judgment.

That's right. I never testified. I didn't even know the case was going on. The judge's decision was based strictly on my report, not my testimony. I didn't get the opportunity to "clear anything up." My report had to stand on its own.

The defendant appealed the case to the state appellate court. No new witnesses get called to testify at this particular type of court proceeding. Instead, the judges review the actions of the trial court and the documentation of the trial. This included my police report. So once again, my report had to stand as an independent document, with no testimony to buttress it—with new eyes looking at it.

The defense attorney argued that the trial court had erred and that my arrest was pre-textual. Upon review, my actions that evening were upheld. The conviction by the trial court was affirmed. The defendant was guilty of possession of methamphetamine. But had I written an unclear report, this may not have been the result. Everything flowed from a clear report. An ambiguous or vague report would have provided the defense attorney with sufficient ammunition to blow holes in the state's case (*my* case, essentially, because I investigated it and made the arrest). Because I never had the opportunity to testify, the prosecutor wouldn't be able to ask me to clarify anything on the witness stand during redirect. She would have to make her arguments strictly from my report, as well.

Did I write the greatest report known to mankind? Hardly. But the report was clear (it was also concise, complete, and accurate, thankfully). And the important point here is that it stood on its own two

---

23 Apparently, the defense attorney thought the facts were on his side, because he was comfortable enough to stipulate. Or, more likely, he thought he saw a weakness in the facts I presented.

feet, despite considerable scrutiny from numerous people. All of your reports should do the same—and they can.

Here's my last word, for now, on this little once-upon-a-time. Do you think that when I wrote this report through bleary, sleepy eyes one March morning in 1995 after working a full graveyard shift that I had any clue it would be looked at by the state appellate court judges three years later? Of course not. I had nary a clue. And you will never know which of *your* reports will have to stand up to extreme scrutiny, be it for a criminal case or some kind of civil litigation. So write all of them so that they will stand up on their own.

End of story.

And look at that. The grammar section is still waiting for us both. Oh well. Let's do it. Drop the puck. Game on.

DID I MENTION THAT GRAMMAR SUCKS?

My motto with regard to grammar is that you should use proper or best grammar in your police report. I'll touch on some basic grammar rules that are relevant to report writing. I'll tell you what I believe is proper or best for report writing. But you're not going to learn English grammar in its entirety here. That is too large a task for a book like this—even with Doug's help.[24]

Start by writing in complete sentences. Every sentence must have at least a noun and a verb. A noun and a verb make the sentence a complete sentence. You don't want to write fragmentary sentences, only complete ones.

`"Threw the ball"` is not a complete sentence. It is only a phrase. That phrase lacks a noun/subject. In other words, *who or what* threw the ball?

`"Willie Mays threw the ball"` *is* a complete sentence. *Willie Mays* is the noun (subject) and *threw* is the verb. The sentence is technically complete at that point. The rest of the sentence (*the ball*) includes the direct object, which is what was affected by the action that the noun/subject took.

---

24 Doug is a grammar guru. Seriously. Totally into grammar. A grammar animal.

In another example, **"The baseball player"** is not a complete sentence. It lacks a verb; what action did the baseball player take?

"The baseball player ran to first base" *is* a complete sentence. It has the verb *ran*. Now we have the action that the subject performed (as well as a little more information about where he ran).

Remember, a sentence must have a noun and a verb to be a complete sentence.

Of course, the opposite of an incomplete sentence is a run-on sentence. This is something else to avoid. A run-on sentence is one that continues and continues, using commas and the word *and* and any other means to keep going and going and going, like the Energizer Bunny, who just never stops but instead keeps pounding away at that drum until his pink, fuzzy little arms must be exhausted and..., and..., and....

See what I mean? It's like your one friend who won't ever shut up, even when he says he's shutting up. Don't be that guy.

Another writer[25] once told me that *and* is a very big word. People frequently use it to connect sentences that really should be two separate sentences. If you think you might have a run-on sentence, look for the word *and* somewhere in the middle. That is often a good place to drop in a period and create two sentences instead of one. For example,

I opened the door to the investigator's office and I picked up the Robertson case file.

versus

I opened the door to the investigator's office. I picked up the Robertson case file.

The same is true with commas. A comma is primarily used to divide clauses. *However, writers, sometimes, like to sprinkle commas, throughout sentences, like pepper.* This last sentence is a perfect example. A simple rule regarding commas is "if in doubt, leave it out." People also tend to use commas to connect sentences when periods are what they should have used. This doesn't just create a run-on sentence; it also creates a grammatically incorrect sentence most times. Besides that, two short sentences are easier to read than one long one. For example,

---

25 Billy Bourg, out of Louisiana. He's a crime writer and a cop.

```
I asked Wilma if she knew who took her purse,
she said no.
```

This should read,

```
I asked Wilma if she knew who took her purse.
She said no.
```

Or, depending on the context,

```
I asked Wilma if she knew who took her purse,
but she said no.
```

In any event, the first example is an instance in which the comma is being used as a period. A comma isn't a period. A period is a period. A comma is used to separate clauses or items in a list or to indicate a natural pause in the sentence (but that pause still has to be grammatically correct).

Look at it this way. You use a screwdriver to insert a screw, right? And you use a hammer to drive a nail. Neither tool is appropriate for the opposite job. In fact, both are pretty awkward if you try to use them incorrectly. The same applies with punctuation. Use the right tool for the job.

MAN, AM I EVER TENSE

Moving along, always write in the past tense. What is the *past tense*? It is writing about things that have already happened. The present tense is writing about things that are happening now. The future tense is writing about things that will happen in the future.

A police report should be written in the past tense. Why? Logically, because the events already occurred, right? Of course they did. Unless you were standing there, dictating events as they unfolded, the report shouldn't be in the present tense. And unless you're the Amazing Muzatko and can accurately predict police events that will happen the next day, the report shouldn't be in the future tense.

Past tense. That is where your report lives. I *went* to the store. I *played* hockey. I *cleaned* the garage. I *arrested* Sam. In each of these sentences, it is clear that the action has already occurred.

You might be shaking your head right now, thinking, "Why is he spending three paragraphs on this? One sentence should handle this: *write in the past tense.*" You'd think so, wouldn't you? But unfortunately, that's not the case. Though I have never seen an officer turn in a report written in the future tense,[26] it is not uncommon for officers to occasionally slip into forms of the present test. This is usually because we do this at times in our spoken communication. More than once, I've read something like, **"After I deflected his punch, I move into a defensive posture and deliver two closed fist strikes to the midsection."** In this example, the officer began the sentence appropriately enough in the past tense but then slipped into the present tense when further describing his actions.

This is the instinctive storyteller in us, I believe. By putting it in the present tense, we increase the immediacy of it and the tension. Works *great* in oral presentations. In a police report, not so much. Just be aware of this during the revision process, and you'll catch it most times.

A more common mistake is the use of the past progressive. Whenever you see the word *was* followed by a verb that ends in *-ing,* you are dealing with the past progressive. *I was struggling to grab his wrist* is an example of past progressive. This form is generally not as clear as *I struggled to grab his wrist.* There are some exceptions. You might write, *I was struggling to grab his wrist when he punched me in the stomach* in order to show the first action that was occurring when another, second action was completed. In this instance, though, it wouldn't be as good to write, *I was struggling to grab his wrist when he was punching me.* It isn't as clear. In fact, it starts to get a little muddy. It sounds like activity that is frequent and continuous, instead of what actually happened.

Thus, the clearest structure might be to write, *As I struggled to grab his wrist, he punched me.* This avoids the progressive entirely.

You may notice that all of those sentences are written in the *first person.* What does that mean? It refers to the speaker. In the preceding sentences, *I* am describing the events. *I* am the narrator. Pronouns such as *I* and *we* are used in the first person.

---

26 If I ever see an Officer Nostradamus on the roster, though, I might check out some of his reports. Just to see.

Your reports should all be in the first person. After all, *you* are reporting the events of *your* investigations.

Not to confuse things, but *you* is the pronoun for the second person. How about the third person? *He, she, they.*

In literature, it is always a conscious choice about which person and viewpoint the author chooses to employ in telling his story. You might see it in the third person (**"Marlowe sat at his desk and waited"**) or the first person (**"I sat and my desk and waited"**). On rare, experimental occasions, you might read a work of fiction in the second person[27] (**"You sat at your desk and waited"**[28]). But you should never see a police report told from any vantage point other than the first person. It is your report. Take center stage.

In the not-so-distant past, many officers used the patented phrase, **"This officer did."** A report might read, **"This officer did respond to the hospital."** I think the reason for this may have been to emphasize objectivity. It could also have been an attempt to appear more professional and clinical. I think it sounds kinda clunky myself. But even if it does accomplish what was intended, it comes at the expense of clarity and simplicity.[29] In today's world, the sentence should read, **"I responded to the hospital."**

It is a matter of clarity.

What officers are doing with the "This Officer Did" model is referring to themselves in the third person. Taken further, this model would change the sentence to read, **"Officer Brown did respond to the hospital."** Now, when you consider that it is Officer Brown who is writing the report, you can see where it is not as clear as simply writing, **"I responded to the hospital."**

---

27 *Bright Lights, Big City* by Jay McInerney is one example. He wrote another great novel called *Ransom*. If you can find it, it is a great read. It's not written in the second person, though.

28 In the few instances in which I've seen this done, the writer usually puts the novel in the present tense, too. So the sentence reads, *You sit at your desk and wait.*

29 I long ago gave up trying to convince older officers to change from this model to the newer, simpler model of using "I" instead of "this officer." With the exception of this Paleolithic technique, most of them write better reports than most of the younger officers, anyway.

ACTIVE VERSUS PASSIVE VOICE

In addition to writing your reports in the past tense and in the first person, reports should also be in the *active voice*. This is where students usually say, "Active *what*?" Active voice is a little confusing, but it is really just a matter of word order. Compare the following:

1. *Passive.* `Sam was fought with by me. Sam was subdued and arrested by me. He was then taken to jail.`

2. *Active.* `Sam fought with me. I subdued and arrested him. I then took him to jail.`

Which method is clearer? The first sentence **(Sam was fought with by me)**, in particular, is less ambiguous in number two than in example one. In the passive construct, the implication is that the officer initiated the fight, when in fact it was Sam.

For a bit of a grammatical explanation, it goes like this. In active voice, the subject of the sentence takes an action upon the direct object. In passive voice, the structure is reversed. The direct object has an action taken upon it by the subject.

Passive voice is generally considered a weaker structure. It is also less clear. Often the "by me" is omitted in common speech, so it becomes even more confusing. **"Sam was arrested."** By whom? Who is responsible?

Using the active voice, on the other hand, leaves little doubt as to who took what action. *Who* arrested Sam? *I* did.

This can be particularly important in law enforcement circles when it comes to decision making. Take this arrest scenario regarding Sam, for example. Officers can confer all day long regarding the facts of the case and the existence of probable cause, if they want to. Each officer can voice his opinion. But ultimately, *an officer* will make the decision that probable cause (PC) exists and *an officer* will arrest Sam. It might be Officer Brown, or it might be the supervisor on scene; but the decision that PC exists and an arrest must be made is a singular one. That is why I cringe when I read sentences in police reports like, **"I conferred with Officer Gomez and Sgt. McGee. It was determined that probable cause existed for burglary. Sam was arrested and booked into jail.**

Does anyone see some ambiguity there? Who decided that PC existed? Who made the arrest?

How about **"I conferred with Officer Gomez and Sgt. McGee. I determined that probable cause existed for burglary. I arrested Sam and booked him into jail"**?

Passive voice is a haven for ambiguity. That's why finger-pointers love it so much. A person who loves to pass the buck and shirk responsibility absolutely adores passive voice, because it allows him to paint every decision as a committee decision and every action as a group action. Even when he's alone, passive voice allows him to portray events as just sort of happening, almost by chance.

While at times this might seem like a small distinction (and in some sentences, it is), this concept is important. We can't afford to be ambiguous in our reports. Much will be made of any ambiguity. As a patrol officer, you will go on a number of very involved, confusing calls with multiple civilian and police participants.[30] It is critical to be clear about who did what (and when, of course), including gathering information that leads toward probable cause and decisions such as whether to make an arrest. The use of active voice instead of passive keeps those events clear to the reader.

Also, imagine if you wrote a report full of passive sentence construction that led to considerable ambiguity surrounding the events. Then imagine being on the stand a year or more later while the defense attorney makes much hay out of each one of the slightest ambiguities that you gift wrapped for him by using the passive voice construct. The inference he'll make when you have to explain a lot of critical things on the witness stand that aren't clear in your report is that you are "testi-lying," not testifying.

Obviously, that's not the way we want it to go. As a police officer, you need to take responsibility for every action you make out there. And you have to be clear that it is *your* decision and *your* action. One way to be clear about that is to write your reports in the active voice.

How do you cut out passive voice? Look for the verb *was* in all its forms. Eight times out of ten, you'll have your culprit. Reword the sentence by making the subject and the verb the highlight of the sentence,

---

30 In my agency, we call them "cluster calls." The derivation of that term comes from another phrase that is considerably less polite.

not the direct object. As in the preceding example, *Sam was fought with by me* becomes *Sam fought with me.*

One might argue that *I fought with Sam* would be even better. On strictly technical terms, that is probably correct. However, words are important—and not just word choice but word order. Word choice and word order create meaning.

Who is driving these events? Sam is—by not complying with lawful, verbal requests to surrender. So he is fighting with the officer, not the other way around. Words matter. They paint a picture. Just be careful how you fling the paint. Careless use and you have Jackson Pollock instead of Da Vinci.

As an aside, writers generally avoid passive voice like the plague in fiction, too. It's just not very dynamic. Because you've been slogging through some pretty dry stuff for a few pages, let me give you a slight chuckle with an example of how bad passive voice can be in a work of fiction:

> The room was walked into by a man by whom strong, handsome features were had. A woman was met by him. The bed was lain upon by him. The bed was lain upon by her. Clothing was removed from them both. Sex was had. Climax was achieved. Afterward, cigarettes were smoked by them. Suddenly, the door was opened by the husband of the woman by whom the bed was lain upon. A gun was held by him. Some screams were screamed and angry words were exchanged. Jealousy was felt by the man by whom the gun was held. Firing of the gun was done by him. The flying of bullets took place. Impact was felt by bodies. The floor was hit by bodies. Remorse was then felt by the man by whom the gun was held.
>
> The gun was turned upon himself.[31]

Pretty gripping stuff, huh? Edgar Award winning prose, no doubt.

---

31 John Vorhaus in *The Comic Toolbox.*

Is that to say that the verb *was* always indicates passive voice? No. Remember, it has to do with who is taking the action upon whom. Is passive voice always wrong? No, not always. Every rule has exceptions. An occasional situation may be easier to describe in passive voice. If so, use it. But don't use it to confuse or out of laziness. Use it purposefully and in order to be clearer.

CHANGE IT UP

The last thing about grammar that I want to leave you with is more stylistic than it is a rigid rule. When writing your report, you should change paragraphs[32] when you change topics.

How long should a paragraph be? When do you change paragraphs in a report? There is no ironclad answer to this. A general rule of thumb is to change paragraphs whenever you change ideas. If there is a shift in topic, definitely change paragraphs. How drastic or how subtle a shift is depends on the length and detail of the work. There doesn't have to be a radical change. In fact, there can be subtle changes within one general idea.

Generally, a reader is put off by an overlong paragraph. It's hard on the eyes.

THE END IS JUST THE BEGINNING

Well, we've reached the end of the chapter on the CLEAR pillar. It will probably prove to be the longest chapter of this book, because clarity is hugely important in police report writing. Additionally, we've already broached some topics that we'll be revisiting during our examination of the other three pillars. That'll make things go faster.

Remember, ladies and gentlemen, in order to be of any use, your report must be CLEAR.

Are *we* clear?

Crystal?

Good. Let's move on.

---

32 And double-space between those paragraphs, please.

Photo courtesy of M. J. Rose Images.

Police car closeup.

EXERCISES

Practice Makes...Better

Because one of the only ways to get better at writing is to write, we include some suggested writing exercises at the end of each of the four pillar chapters. Some are designed to beef up your writing skills in general. Others are focused more directly on police reports.

I'm no dummy. I know that most people aren't going to do these unless they're part of a class assignment. That's fine. After all, you know your learning patterns better than I do. You know how much work you need on reports. So maybe you do them or maybe you don't. What I *do* know is that if you choose to do these exercises, they *will* help.

Exercises to Help with Being CLEAR

1. Watch your favorite movie or episode of a television show. Write what occurred. Remember that whoever is reading it doesn't know anything about this show, so you have to be clear about what happened. Show your paragraph to someone who hasn't seen the movie or show and ask that person if your paragraph is *clear*.

2. Try doing exercise 1 using an episode from the *COPS* television series. This may be hard to do because the *COPS* episodes sometimes

lack some of the important details. Do the best you can and add in what you think is missing to help with the clarity.

3. Spelling is always a problem. Following is a list of frequently mis-spelled words (particularly in law enforcement circles). Study them and quiz yourself, because you'll see them again.

abduction	ceiling	occurrence	premises	straight
accessories	exaggerating	offense	prosecutor	strangulation
acquitted	fictitious	opinion	sabotage	subpoena
altercation	harassment	paid	scene	succession
apparatus	inferred	patrolling	scent	summons
approximately	jeopardize	penalize	seize	surrender
arson	libel	personal	sentence	suspect
belief	lieutenant	physician	separation	techniques
beneficial	losing	possession	serious	than
bureau	marshal	practical	shining	thorough
category	necessary	precinct	statute	tourniquet

4. Confusing Words. These are just a few words that are often confused in police reports with regard to meaning. Just like the spelling words, study these and quiz yourself, because you'll be dealing with these words throughout your career. The word is in **bold**. The sentence should put the word into meaningful context for you. Additional context is in *italics*.

  a. Stare/stairs

    i. Don't **stare** at people; it's rude. *To look intently and continually at something.*

    ii. Be careful not to fall down the **stairs**. *Steps leading up or down.*

  b. Than/then

    i. Seven is more **than** five. *Regarding things that are relative.*

    ii. Rather **than** go home, he went to a party. *Instead of.*

    iii. He went to the party, **then** he went home. *Related to time or sequence.*

  c. There/they're/their

    i. **There** are three pieces of pizza on the counter. *To be.*

    ii. What did you do over **there**? *Location.*

iii. **They're** [they are] late for the movie. *Contraction of "they are."*

iv. That is **their** house. They've owned it for 10 years. *Possessive.*

d. Principal/principle

    i. He is the **principal** at the high school. *Administrator.*

    ii. The **principal** reason I became a cop was to help people. *Main or primary.*

    iii. This nation was based upon the **principle** of freedom. *Ideal or concept.*

e. Sight/site/cite

    i. If you lose **sight** of the suspect, radio in the last known location. *Related to seeing.*

    ii. The burial **site** was in the forest. *Location.*

    iii. If you don't stop making noise, I will have to **cite** you. *To issue a citation/arrest.*

    iv. If you're going to make a reference, **cite** your source. *List.*

f. Base/bass/bass

    i. The sculpture sits upon its **base**. *Support.*

    ii. Head back to the Army **base**. *Location.*

    iii. The stereo had a heavy **bass**. *Pronounced base. Thumping.*

    iv. I went **bass** fishing. *Type of fish, rhymes with grass.*

g. Board/bored

    i. Write your name up on the **board**. *A surface, a plank.*

    ii. I tried to listen to the lecture but I got **bored**. *An emotional state, not excited.*

h. Your/you're/yore

    i. **Your** job is to fight crime. *Possessive.*

    ii. If **you're** on duty, be alert! *Contraction of "you are."*

    iii. In the days of **yore**. *Long ago.*

i. Weather/whether

    i. What will tomorrow's **weather** be like? *Sunny, snowy.*

    ii. We're going camping **whether** or not you come along. *Alternatives.*

    j. Vain/vein/vane

        i. Carly Simon thought Warren Beatty was quite **vain**. *Narcissistic. Stuck on yourself.*

        ii. Thankfully, it was a **vein** and not an artery. *Blood vessel.*

        iii. The weather **vane** is pointing northeast. *Direction finder.*

    k. To/two/too

        i. I'm going **to** a concert. *Preposition indicating movement.*

        ii. I have **two** hands. *Number.*

        iii. You have them, **too**. *Also.*

5. Crime and Evidence in Action

    a. Access the Crime and Evidence in Action CD.

    b. Log in as yourself. Select the burglary case. Select phase one (patrol officer).

    c. Conduct the investigation, taking careful notes.

    d. Complete a report based upon your investigation. Focus especially upon the element of CLARITY in your report.

    e. **To access the example of this report, log in to** <u>www.cengagebrain</u> <u>.com</u> **and access the website that accompanies this book.** Compare your report to the example report.

6. Cengage Learning Criminal Justice Media Library

    a. Access the "Arrest" module under Fundamentals of Criminal Justice.

    b. Complete the brief exercise.

    c. Once you have the correct answers in the correct column, your assignment is: Give a written example of the importance of being CLEAR when you are involved in suspect contacts (stop versus arrest). What specific pitfalls might you face if you are unclear about the listed elements in this exercise?

7. Practice on the following example of a (poor) burglary report. Go through and mark anything that doesn't subscribe to the elements of the CLEAR pillar that we've discussed in this chapter. Revise accordingly. Save your revised, working copy; we'll use it again!

EXAMPLE BURGLARY REPORT

On an unusually sunny Sunday afternoon in February (the 7th to be exact) of the year 2010, I was sent by police radio via a 911 call to the 911 call center to a burglary of a house at 2914 East Indiana in the City and County of Spokane in the great state of Washington. According to the clock on my car radio, I received the call at 1530 hours but the call history actually shows the time I received the call was 1532 hours. Radio told me the 911 operator in the 911 call center had told them the person who had called 911 had told them their house had been broken into while they were gone over the weekend (not that I could blame them for being gone, it was so nice!) but didn't believe the suspects were still in the house.

As it was such a nice day and the suspects were no longer in the process of burglarizing the house, I took my time and drove the speed limit to the call. I wanted to make sure I enjoyed the sunny afternoon as much as possible. While on my way to the call, I went out of my way to drive by Garry Park so I could see all of the families out there enjoying themselves. When I drove by, I saw a large group of people had a co-ed softball going. I was really bummed because I enjoy playing as well but was unable to because of work. Oh well, I had the next weekend off.

I drove onto the 2900 block of East Indiana from the west. I thought this was a good safety tactic since the sun was behind me and wouldn't be in my eyes as I approached. The late afternoon sun can really be harsh sometimes. When I finally did get to the house, I saw it was a beautiful two tone brown Craftsman style house with a deep, rich brown colored front door. The house had an approx. three foot light brown picket fence surrounding it (except for the driveway portion of course). The best part was that the yard was already starting to turn green! I can't wait until spring.

I approached the house by walking up the driveway. The driveway was a pretty standard concrete driveway set up for a three car garage. I turned right towards the front door and entered the yard and fenced area through a small gate. I made sure to close the gate after me in case they had animals they didn't want to escape the yard. I walked up two aggregate concrete steps onto the front porch (which was also aggregated concrete). I looked on both sides of the brown front door for a doorbell. When I was unable to locate one, I knocked on the door exactly three times. I made sure not to strike the door too loudly so I wouldn't startle anyone inside.

The door was answered by a somewhat attractive female (if you like blondes). She was a full-bodied woman who looked like she was well taken care of. I asked her if she was the resident of the home. She told me she was. I asked her what her name was. She told me her name was Susannah Rettinghouse. I thought that was a strange name but the way she said it really made it sound nice. I made sure I asked her to correctly spell her name because of all of the variations of her first name. I wanted to make sure I had it correct.

Mrs. Susannah Rettinghouse told me she and her husband, Mr. Brian Rettinghouse, had been out of town over the weekend visiting family. She said they left on Friday February 5th, 2010 at "1500 hours." She said they had gone to the town of Ellensburg in the central part of Washington State to attend a wedding for their niece. When I commented on the length of the drive, she said that was the reason they had driven their 2009 Honda Accord four door (WA plate #123ABC) instead of their 2008 Chevy Yukon Denali (WA plate #987UBI). She said it just

(continued)

EXAMPLE BURGLARY REPORT (CONTINUED)

She said Mr. Rettinghouse stayed in Ellensburg to cover her niece's business while she is on her honeymoon and she drove home alone.

Susanna told me when she returned that morning, she pulled into her driveway so she could park her car in one of the stalls (the one closest to the house) in the three car garage. She said after she grabbed her purse, she exited her car and shut the door. She said she walked in the house through the door leading from the garage into the kitchen area. She said she immediately stopped because she saw several of her kitchen drawers and cabinets standing open. She said she also could see her double paned insulated glass sliding glass door in the dining room standing open. She said she could tell it was open because the white sheer curtain was blowing slightly inward. She said she backed out of the house and called 911. She said she got tired of waiting for the police to arrive so she went into the house to see if anyone was still inside. I told her this was a really dumb thing for her to do. What if she had found someone and became severely injured! She said she didn't find anyone inside the house.

Mrs. Wateringhouse and I walked through the residence to identify if anything was missing. There were many things of value contained within the house. The people who lived there are obviously well to do and deserved the attention of police services. When we entered the master bedroom, I saw most of the dresser drawers were pulled out and ransacked. Susannah said she was missing approx. fifteen hundred and seventy dollars from inside one of the drawers. She said she was saving the money for a rainy day. She said she didn't believe anything else was missing.

I looked at the sliding glass door for evidence of damage. I was unable to locate any. Susannah told me her teenage son, Jeffery Rettinghouse, sometimes forgets to lock the door. She said she didn't know where he was at right then but mentioned he had stayed in Spokane with her parents that weekend. She said her parents only live a few blocks away. She said he had been in trouble recently for taking things that didn't belong to him.

While standing in the kitchen area, Susannah offered me a cold soft drink or iced tea. I immediately refused because I didn't want to accept any type of gratuity. It was at that point Susannah pointed to an empty pop can on her kitchen counter and stated, "That wasn't there when we left!" I collected the pop can as evidence, securing it in a paper bag in the trunk of my police car.

I took photographs of the empty pop can and ransacked bedroom. I was unable to locate any obvious fingerprints on the point of entry/exit or within the house.

I went next door and spoke to the male neighbor. He told me he had been home all weekend. He said he had heard a noise next door the previous day. He said he had looked over and saw a male walking in the back yard of the house. He watched the male for a few moments but didn't say anything because he assumed it was the boy who lived there. I did not gather any information from him or ask him to describe the male he saw because I figured he could just tell a detective when they follow up on this case.

I gave Susannah a crime victim card with the incident number on it. I asked her to call detectives if she discovered anything else missing. I asked her if there was anything else I could do

(*continued*)

EXAMPLE BURGLARY REPORT (CONTINUED)

for her. She told me no. I clarified that she was 100% OK staying at home by herself. She told me she thought she would be fine. I told her I would stay in the neighborhood the rest of the day to be sure she was OK. She sounded very appreciative of my doing that and asked me to stop by if I needed anything. I told her I would.

At the end of my shift, I cleared the area but didn't see anyone unusual in the area.

CHAPTER 3

CONCISE

STEVE IS COOL (PART I)

CONCISE writing is the second pillar of good report writing.

Writing a concise report is almost an art form. Some officers approach report writing with almost a "throw it all in" mentality. They include anything and everything that they can think of in the report. This makes for a mess. And it isn't professional.

At my agency, the basic police report form used to have boxes for information to be entered on the entire front side and midway down the back page. This left approximately half a page to write the narrative. In most reports, officers were forced to continue their narrative on an additional narrative sheet. However, it was considered something of a badge of honor to finish a report of substance on the second page of the basic report. The key, of course, was that the report also needed to be complete (something we'll discuss in the next lesson).

My buddy and fellow cop, Steve McHugill, was an ace at writing concise reports.[1] In fact, he became something of a minor legend for it. We'd be working on paper sometime in the early morning hours of a graveyard shift and he'd hand me a face sheet. Nothing else, just a face sheet.

"Check this over for me, would ya?" he'd ask.

I'd turn it over and see that it was a "2 of 2" (referring to the pagination). I'd squint. "Where's the rest?" I'd ask, probably because the call had been a domestic dispute or something else equally involved.

"It's all there," he'd say, already pulling out another face sheet and starting to fill it out.

"Impossible," I'd think. "He didn't even use all of the lines on the second page." Then I'd read it. Sure enough, all the relevant facts were there. All of the probable cause was present. There was no fluff. No redundancies. His narrative was as tight as a piano wire.

That's when I'd usually mutter a curse and toss it back to him.

"Show-off," I'd say.

He'd simply smile and continue scratching out another "2 of 2."

---

1   We worked together a lot, Steve and I. Some of my best war stories (which you won't read in these pages, unfortunately) happened when we were teamed up. We made good partners. My reports tended to be a lot longer, though. If you can imagine that.

Steve naturally discovered and developed methods at being concise. I personally think he did it because he hated writing reports.[2] But either way, these are the methods we'll go over in this lesson.

IT ALL TIES TOGETHER—AND A RIVER RUNS THROUGH IT

In some ways, being concise is an extension of clarity. A concise report avoids clutter. Clutter can make a report unclear.

What do I mean by *clutter*? Ask yourself a question about the last book you read. Particularly if it was a novel, did you read every word on every page? No? Why not? Why did you skip parts?

In the fiction realm, clutter is unacceptable. It bores the reader. It might confuse the reader. It definitely reminds the reader that she is reading a book or a story, thus shattering the necessary illusion[3] we need to maintain in books and films. One way to avoid clutter is to make sure that every sentence—indeed, every word!—is absolutely necessary. Every word has a job to do.

The great crime fiction writer Elmore Leonard[4] was once asked why his books were so widely read. Why, the interviewer wanted to know, were they so successful? What did he do to repeatedly write books that people wanted to read? Leonard replied simply, "I try to leave out the parts that people skip."

That statement, at least in fiction, is an excellent explanation of how to be concise. It translates to nonfiction works (such as this book or your police reports) like this: leave out the clutter!

But being concise is more than just an issue of clutter. Being concise is a matter of economy. It is a matter of expressing the maximum amount of information in the absolute minimum amount of space.

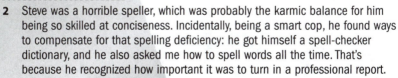

2   Steve was a horrible speller, which was probably the karmic balance for him being so skilled at conciseness. Incidentally, being a smart cop, he found ways to compensate for that spelling deficiency: he got himself a spell-checker dictionary, and he also asked me how to spell words all the time. That's because he recognized how important it was to turn in a professional report.

3   Also known as the "willing suspension of disbelief." Most readers and viewers are rather forgiving on this point, but you never want to push your luck.

4   Never heard of him? He wrote the following novels, many of which were adapted to film: *Hombre, Mr. Majestyk, Stick, Get Shorty,* and several dozen others.

What does *concise* mean? Very simply, it means *get to the point.*

It means only including pertinent facts.

It means writing what happened in a brief, straightforward manner.

Some writers tend to overwrite.[5] They go on and on about something even after the point has been clearly made. This insults your reader and detracts from your message.

How long should a report be? That is a difficult question to quantify. A report should be as long as it needs to be in order to be clear, complete, and accurate—*and no longer.* If it meets these criteria, it is, by definition, concise.

Everything is relative on this point and is topic dependent. A homicide report may run 15 pages and be considered concise, whereas a simple theft case of that same length may be bloated.

In addition to being related to the CLEAR pillar, the CONCISE pillar of report writing is also related to the COMPLETE pillar. The two concepts might seem diametrically opposed or somehow in conflict with each other, but in reality, they are not. A concise report must also be a complete report, and it is entirely possible for the two to be in balance.

If, however, you encounter a situation in which you are unsure whether your report is *concise* enough but you are battling to make sure it is *complete*, always err on the side of completeness. Far less damage is done by minor overwriting than by omitting facts.

Most reports, though, could stand a little bit of healthy trimming. This can usually be accomplished in the revision stage of the writing process.

Take the example in the Robert Redford film *A River Runs Through It*. This movie about fly fishing and brothers (a concise description, you might say) takes place in the early part of the 1900s. The two boys, whose father is a pastor, are home schooled. In one scene, the eldest son brings a page-long essay to his father. The pastor whips out his red grease pencil[6] and begins to mark up the essay rather extensively. Then he hands it back to his son.

"Half as long," he tells the boy and returns to his reading.

5   As much as I love his work, there have been times when I felt Stephen King was doing this; but who am I to criticize, right? He's only sold about eight gajillion books.

6   If you remember what one of those is, I'm impressed. Every session at the academy, fewer and fewer students do. I think that when I ask and absolutely no one remembers, then hell with it. I'll just retire. That very day.

What does he mean by this, do you suppose? He means that he wants his son to convey the same ideas and information but in half the length.

The poor kid goes back to his desk and rewrites the essay. This time, it is half a page long. The pastor slashes it up with the red grease pencil and hands it back to him.

"Half as long," he intones.

The boy sighs and takes the essay back to his desk. When he returns a third time, he has a paragraph written on the page. Nothing more. He hands it to the pastor and waits nervously. The pastor reads it. He makes a couple of marks with his grease pencil. Then he looks down at the boy.

"Very well," he says. "Go on now."

The boy smiles in pure joy. He and his brother go fishing.

Although the character in this movie was only about 8 years old at the time, his father taught him a pair of valuable lessons. He taught him to be concise and to revise.

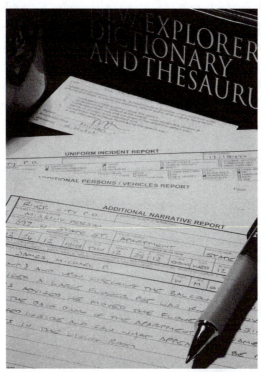

Photo courtesy of M. J. Rose Images.

A concise report may be short but still contains all the relevant facts.

STEVE IS COOL (PART II)[7]

How much information can you delete from a report? *Anything* unnecessary can be deleted. To illustrate this point, consider a Hollywood anecdote.

While filming the action movie *Bullitt*,[8] actor Steve McQueen became involved in an argument with the director, Peter Yates. Throughout the film, McQueen's character is hounded by a corrupt politician, and the politician levies threats at him. In one scene, the script called for a long monologue from McQueen denouncing the politician and putting him in his place. The speech McQueen was to deliver was several pages and a couple of film minutes long.

McQueen didn't want to do the speech. He thought it was too wordy and out of character for the cop he was playing. Finally, Yates became exasperated and asked McQueen what he wanted to say. McQueen canceled out the entire monologue. Then, he wrote in the margin what would become a famous movie quote: "You work your side of the street, and I'll work mine."

This is the beauty of concise writing. Although this single sentence is full of subtext, the meaning and intent of McQueen's character are intact. From a creative standpoint, this compresses all the emotional energy of the exchange into a single powerful statement.

Clearly, this radical of a change is not appropriate for a technical report, which differs significantly from a creative endeavor such as a film. However, this anecdote should highlight the efficacy of conciseness.

THE HOW OF IT

How important is it to be concise? As mentioned previously, a concise report lends itself to clarity. It keeps the readers from focusing on irrelevant matters and allows them to concentrate on the pertinent ones.

A concise report, therefore, saves the reader time. It also saves the writer time from recording unnecessary material. Overall, concise writing lends itself to a more professional report. This is because a concise report has a "clean" feel to it.

7   A different Steve this time. Sorry, McHuges.
8   1968, from Warner Brothers.

The advantage, then, of a concise report is that it ensures economy for both the writer and especially the reader.

How can you make your writing concise?

This is a question that writers in every field struggle with. It can be a daunting task, particularly when you want to ensure completeness. There are, however, strategies you can employ to help you be more concise.

The first strategy is to eliminate unneeded information. If you have included information that is irrelevant to the report, that report is now longer than it needs to be. By definition, this is not concise.

How do you decide what is relevant and what isn't? This is not a function of writing so much as it is a job knowledge issue. A younger officer tends to write longer reports than a veteran officer.[9] Why? Because the veteran has the experience to know what is or may be relevant. She only includes those facts that are necessary to the report. The veteran also has the knowledge and experience to ensure that all pertinent information is in the report, making it complete.

You will have to employ job-specific knowledge, experience, and common sense[10] to decide whether facts in the report should be there or not. Along the way, you can get input from trainers, supervisors, and more experienced peers.

Once you're fairly certain that all the information in your report needs to be there, the next step is to address *how* you are conveying the message. That is a matter of craft rather than specific job knowledge.

CHARLOTTE WAS CONCISE

I have been accused of being verbose. My friends notice it. My coworkers endure it. My wife teaches, and even one of her students[11] pointed it out on an author visit I made to her classroom. So I know it exists as a tendency. Wait, did I say tendency?

Call it my nature and we'll be closer on the mark.

You may even feel at times in this textbook that I've rambled off on a tangent, and I can't say you'd be wrong. But believe it or not, I do

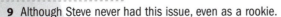

9 Although Steve never had this issue, even as a rookie.

10 As noted frequently in life, common sense is all too uncommon.

11 Personally, I think Elizabeth was a little chatty herself, but are you really going to get into that exchange with a sixth grader? No. They win on cuteness every time.

self-police. I edit. I revise. And I accept further edits and revisions from editors. So the verbosity gets whittled down.

A little.

Lots of people are verbose. Some of them are entertaining and we like listening to them. Comedians, for example. We'll sit and listen to them for an hour-long monologue without complaint. Similarly, if we're in a class that's interesting to us, a lecture is something we can enjoy, even if it is verbose.

But being overly verbose (or morbidly verbose, as I can be) is an enemy of concise writing. If you struggle with this, remember the simple adage of KISS. No, not the hard rock band with the makeup. Not your favorite radio station, either. No, I mean "Keep It Simple, Stupid."

Writing as simply as you can lends itself to being concise (the reverse is also true).

Example?

One day, a verbose farmer and a concise farmer set up shop at the farmer's livestock market. A buyer comes along and asks the verbose farmer, "What are you selling today?"

The verbose farmer says, "A genus of even-toed mammal ungulates, often wild, but mostly raised domestically throughout the world and bred primarily for providing meat and meat by-products from their flesh. They have a short body covered in thick, coarse hair, often exceed 400 pounds in weight, and are often immediately known by sight because of a large nose called a 'snout' on their face, which is used to dig up crops by their roots, thus causing much destruction."[12]

The buyer cocks an eyebrow and glances over at the concise farmer. "And you?"

The concise farmer smiles and says, "Pigs."

NEVER THE TWAIN SHALL MEET

Overly long sentences[13] are a classic sign of a report that is not concise. If a sentence is too long, the danger always exists that clarity will suffer as the reader gets lost in the twists and turns of that sentence. It takes a good

---

12 Thank you to Officer Tim Moses for this example.

13 Not to be confused with a run-on sentence, which is more of a grammatical error. Still, both kinds of sentences can be unclear.

writer to roll out a long sentence and still get her meaning across. Of course, it takes a better writer to cut up that sentence into a more concise message.

That might sound funny at first. It takes a better writer to write something shorter? Yes. Let's explore this just for a moment.

The well-known American humorist and writer Mark Twain is said to have had an exchange in which a magazine editor telegraphed him and asked for 30 pages in two days. Twain said he could do the job. The editor telegraphed him back and asked for only two pages instead. Twain wrote him that he could give him 30 pages in two days, but if the editor wanted only two pages, Twain needed 30 days for that task.[14]

Twain, incidentally, had a number of rules about writing. Because they also apply to report writing, I'll include them here. According to Twain, an author should:

- Say what he is proposing to say, not merely come near it.

- Use the right word, not its second cousin.

- Eschew surplusage.

- Not omit necessary details.

- Avoid slovenliness of form.

- Use good grammar.

- Employ a simple, straightforward style.

Do you see anything familiar in that list? Things that might refer to clarity?

Anything about being concise? Complete? Accurate?

MORE HOW

Getting back to the *how*—how do you know if your sentence is too long?

For starters, take a look at it. Is it three lines of text? An entire paragraph? Does your report contain long blocks of uninterrupted text? If so, you might be writing sentences that are too long.

---

14 Again on the subject of being concise, Twain is also often credited with saying, "I'm sorry this letter is so long, but I did not have time to make it shorter." Blaise Pascal actually said this, however.

Do your sentences contain a high frequency of commas that separate clauses? If so, those might better be divided into two separate sentences.

Do you use the word *and* a lot? As we discussed last chapter, *and* can be a very big word. Frequently, it is used to connect a pair of sentences that would be better as complete sentences on their own. Although this may not make your report more concise with regard to word count, it will be stylistically more concise.

Is your sentence aimed at a single purpose or are you trying to accomplish more than one thing with a single sentence? If the latter is the case, your sentence will likely be longer (and meandering). Think of each sentence as a particular goal. A baseball analogy might be: *Swing the bat. Hit the ball. Run the bases. Score a run. Win the game. Get a new contract.* All of these are separate sentences because they are all focused on a particular goal. Sure, the player in question might have an ultimate goal in mind (a new contract), but it wouldn't do to put all six of these goals in a single sentence. Break the purposes down to their singular nature.[15] Each sentence has a goal or a point (*swing the bat, hit the ball*). If you're bunching several goals into one sentence, you're going to have longer, confusing sentences. These are not concise or complete.

Though we discussed this in the previous lesson, I'll repeat it here: the use of passive voice is something you should avoid. Passive voice is not nearly as clear, but it is also frequently wordier than the active voice.

For example:

Passive: The ball was kicked by me.

Active: I kicked the ball.

Even though the word count is only different by two words, the active voice is much clearer and more concise.

Another way to be more concise is to avoid redundancy and to cut out potato chip words.

What is *redundancy*? To answer that question, please refer to the Department of Redundancy Department.

Did you just raise your eyebrows and say, "Huh?" Good. Redundancy is essentially unnecessary, repeated information. It can be something as simple as, *I went to the concert and the concert was very fun when I went.*

---

15 Depending on what you're writing, you might break things down further. How do you hold the bat? What are the mechanics of the swing? These details are focused on even finer points, and so each sentence has a small goal.

Write instead, *I went to the concert. It was fun.* Or even more concise, *The concert was fun.* It can easily be inferred that because you are relating that it was fun, you went to the show. If it were otherwise, you would specify so. For example, *Bruce told me that the concert was fun.*

What are *potato chip words*? Well, potato chips have long been demonized by nutritional experts as being full of "empty" calories and therefore bad for you. There are words like that, too. Don't let them creep into your writing.

Want an example? OK. How about *very*? *Very* is a weak adverb. It is empty, bringing to the table only a matter of degree without context. Furthermore, it relies completely on the word it is modifying. Essentially, it is the lazy man's modifier. How do you avoid it? Instead of saying *very ugly,* say *hideous.* Instead of saying *very loud,* say *deafening.*

In both cases, the word I substituted is more evocative. It paints a clearer picture. Plus, it is one word instead of two.

Still not sold on *very*? Here's what Mark Twain said about it: "Substitute 'damn' every time you're inclined to write 'very'. Your editor will delete it and the writing will be just as it should be."

Very isn't the only potato chip word out there. Each word must pull its own weight. It must serve a purpose. If it doesn't, cut it.

Does cutting a word here and there really matter? Does it work?

It does. There have been times when I have had a short story that was over the particular word count for a specific market. The limit might be 5,000 words, for example, and my story was 5,500 words. If I really

Avoid "potato chip words."

Photo courtesy of M. J. Rose Images.

wanted to get that story at least considered by that market, I needed to trim about 10 percent of the word count. Often, as I went through line by line looking for words to trim, simple changes like the ones I mentioned above made a big difference. Getting rid of passive voice, redundant words, or words that don't pull their own weight usually got my word count down. Not only that, but the result was a tighter story.

In the fiction-writing world, being able to cut one's own work is a necessity. It is also extraordinarily painful. Cutting out a phrase that you really like or even a scene that seems like a winner on its own can be difficult. They call it "killing your darlings," in fact. It can be positively heartbreaking. But it is essential that you're willing to cut small pieces in the interests of the success of whole work.[16]

What does this have to do with report writing? Nothing more than to point out that being concise may be difficult, but it is important.

A TRIP TO THE HOSPITAL

Let's look at an example. Here is a passage from a police report that could stand some editing for conciseness.

> I responded to Sacred Heart Medical Center, driving through downtown to get there. Upon arrival, I parked my car and entered the emergency room, which is located on the southwest corner of the building underneath next to what used to be the cafeteria. Nurse Baker was contacted and did advise me of the presence of a subject who had a warrant and was identified as John Trapper, who was in room 16 at the end of the hall. In addition to the warrant, I was advised by Nurse Baker that John Trapper had also assaulted another nurse who is named Margaret Burns. Nurse Baker has been a nurse for five years and is single. Nurse Burns, however, has been a nurse for almost 30 years and is a widow. Therefore, I went down the hall to room 16 to arrest John

16 As Spock said, the needs of the many outweigh the needs of the few—or the one.

Trapper. He was sitting on the bed when I walked
into room 16. He was ordered to turn around and
put his hands on his head and when he'd done
that, he was handcuffed and I took him to jail.

Pretty bloated, huh? Let's break down this passage in small chunks at
a time.

I responded to Sacred Heart Medical Center,
driving through downtown to get there.

Who cares about the route you took? If there were some particular,
relevant reason for that fact being there, then it should be explained in the
text. Because there isn't, delete that clause and put a period after **Center**.

Upon arrival, I parked my car and entered
the emergency room, which is located on the
southwest corner of the building underneath
next to what used to be the cafeteria.

Again, how relevant is most of this information? If there is any relevance
to the facts in this sentence, the relevance must be demonstrated or the
sentence should be deleted. In this case, everything except the first two words
can be excised. Those two words can be added to the next sentence for context: **Upon arrival, Nurse Baker was contacted. . . .** Of
course, there are problems with that sentence, too, as we'll see.

Nurse Baker was contacted and did advise me
of the presence of a subject who had a warrant and was identified as John Trapper, who
was in room 16 at the end of the hall.

The first problem with this sentence is the use of passive voice. The
first example of this is, **Nurse Baker was contacted.** Who contacted her? Well, it is implied that the narrator did, but this hearkens back
to the reason not to use passive voice for purposes of clarity. This should
begin instead, **I contacted Nurse Baker. . . .**

Another issue with this sentence is that it is overly long. It is a classic
example of using commas and the word *and* to extend a sentence instead
of using a period.

The sentence can be reworked into two shorter sentences. Some re-
wording is necessary, too, in order to avoid redundancy. The patient is
alternatively referred to as a **subject** and then by name and by the fact
that he has a warrant. This isn't clear, nor is it concise.

Instead, let's write:

> `Upon arrival, I contacted Nurse Baker in the`
> `emergency room. She advised me that John`
> `Trapper was in room 16. Trapper had a warrant.`

The next sentence also has some redundancy. For instance, we already know that Trapper has a warrant, so the opening clause can go.

> `In addition to the warrant, I was advised by`
> `Nurse Baker that John Trapper had also assaulted`
> `another nurse who is named Margaret Burns.`

Once again, we have passive voice (`I was advised by Nurse Baker`). Further, the phrase regarding the assault is awkward. Instead, it could better read:

> `Nurse Baker advised`[17] `that Trapper had also`
> `assaulted Nurse Margaret Burns.`

The next two sentences are ridiculously unnecessary:

> `Nurse Baker has been a nurse for five years`
> `and is single. Nurse Burns, however, has been`
> `a nurse for almost 30 years and is a widow.`

There may be instances in which those facts are relevant, but there is nothing here to support that. Maybe if you work for the nurse's labor union, then their seniority would matter. Or if, instead of the police department, you worked for Dating.com, then it might matter what each one's marital status is. Because we're writing a police report, dump both sentences.

Using the word *therefore* is unnecessary here and actually confusing. It denotes an action that is taken based on previous information or actions.

> `Therefore, I went down the hall to room 16`
> `to arrest John Trapper.`

A better structure might be:

> `I contacted Trapper in room 16.`

---

17 As a side note, police officers tend to overuse certain words in their reports. *Advised* is one of them. Like any other useful word, there's nothing wrong with saying *advised,* but try to avoid overuse. It is distracting.

Even the inclusion of "room 16" may be considered redundant by some writers.

```
He was sitting on the bed when I walked into
room 16.
```

Is this relevant? Again, there's nothing within the report that would make it seem so. If whether he was sitting, standing, or lying down is relevant, fine. Do we need to specify room 16? No, not if it was specified in the previous sentence. That sort of redundancy is one form of the "clutter" we talked about earlier.

```
He was ordered to turn around and put his
hands on his head and when he'd done that, he
was handcuffed and I took him to jail.
```

Once again, we have several issues with this final sentence. There is significant use of passive voice. This is a good example of how passive voice makes things sound like they "just happened." *Who* ordered Trapper? *Who* handcuffed him?

A second issue is that the word *and* is used to connect sentences. It might better read:

```
I ordered him to turn away from me and to put
his hands on his head. He did. I handcuffed
him and took him to jail.
```

So, how should this passage look? Well, not addressing any issues other than being as concise as possible, let's see how an improved final draft might look:

```
I responded to Sacred Heart Medical Center.
Upon arrival, I contacted Nurse Baker in the
emergency room. She advised me that John Trap-
per was in room 16. Trapper had a warrant. Nurse
Baker advised that Trapper had also assaulted
Nurse Margaret Burns. I contacted Trapper in
room 16. I ordered him to turn away from me and
to put his hands on his head. He did. I hand-
cuffed him and took him to jail.
```

Note that the revised passage is considerably shorter (74 words instead of 182). It is also much "cleaner" because it doesn't contain any unnecessary facts. The sentences are shorter. Each sentence has a particular purpose and accomplishes that purpose.

If you apply this type of analytical approach to your writing, you can make your reports more concise.

True to its nature, this chapter on CONCISE is only about one-third the length of the CLEAR chapter. Isn't that fitting?

Now we move on to the reputed antithesis of CONCISE—your friend and mine, COMPLETE.

Photo courtesy of M. J. Rose Images.

EXERCISES

1. As a variation on the exercise from the last chapter, watch your favorite movie or episode of a television show (a different one this time). Write what occurred, but this time imagine that you're striving for conciseness without being woefully incomplete. Once again, remember that whoever is reading your description doesn't know anything about this show, so you have to be clear about what happened. Show your paragraph to someone who hasn't seen the movie or show and ask that person if your paragraph is concise (while still clear and complete).

2. Revise your report from Chapter 2 to be more concise.

3. Find an article in the newspaper or a magazine. Choose a few paragraphs to work with. Pare them down as best you can to make the piece more concise, without losing the impact that was the intent of the writer. This exercise is a little harder because the paragraph you're starting with has already supposedly been edited by professionals. But give it a go. You'll find that even professionals fall prey to the same mistakes you do.

4. Crime and Evidence in Action

   a. Access the Crime and Evidence in Action CD.

   b. Log in as yourself. Select the domestic violence case. Select phase one (patrol officer).

   c. Conduct the investigation, taking careful notes.

   d. Complete a report based on your investigation. Focus especially on the element of CLARITY in your report.

   e. **To access the example of this report, log in to <u>www.cengagebrain</u><u>.com</u> and access the website that accompanies this book.** Compare your report to the example report.

5. Cengage Learning Criminal Justice Media Library

   a. Access "Philadelphia Violence" under Policing.

   b. View the video.

   c. Write a *concise* description of the problem that the city of Philadelphia is facing, the response its police department has taken, and the results.

6. Revise your working copy of the example burglary report from Chapter 2 to be more concise. Save your copy; we'll be using it again!

7. Spelling—always spelling. Does it help with being concise? Nope. But it is always an issue, so here are some more commonly misspelled words for you. Study them and quiz yourself, because you'll see them again.

accident	definitely	indictment	receive
achievement	describe	interrogate	recommend
assistance	disastrous	intoxication	referred
burglary	disposition	miscellaneous	repetition
coercion	embezzlement	noticeable	rhythm
collision	environment	ordinance	serial

conspiracy	exaggerate	peculiar	transferred
commission	existent	privilege	truancy
complainant	explanation	procedure	vagrancy
confidential	fascinate	profession	villain
conviction	fraudulent	prominent	woman
counterfeit	haphazard	prostitution	writing
defendant	indict	pursuit	

8. Confusing Words. These are just a few words that are often confused in police reports with regard to meaning. Just like the spelling words, study these and quiz yourself, because you'll be dealing with these words throughout your career. The word is in **bold**. The sentence should put the word into meaningful context for you. Additional context is in *italics*.

   a. Break/brake

      i. Don't drop the eggs or they will **break.** *Destruction.*

      ii. To slow down, apply the **brake.** *Slow down.*

   b. Seen/scene

      i. When was the suspect last **seen** ? *Visual.*

      ii. Make sure you keep a tight perimeter around the crime **scene.** *The actual location.*

   c. Ceiling/sealing

      i. Look up when you're indoors and you'll see the **ceiling.** *A thing.*

      ii. I licked the envelope, **sealing** it. *A verb.*

   d. Affect/effect

      i. How much did his father's death **affect** him? *Verb.*

      ii. We tracked him down and **effected** his arrest. *Also a verb—to cause or make happen.*

      iii. What was the **effect** of his arrest? *Cause or result.*

      iv. Did you collect his personal **effects** ? *Items, belongings.*

   e. Sense/cents

      i. In police work, it helps to have common **sense.** *Native intelligence. Also used to mean "to feel" or otherwise be aware of something.*

      ii. I wrote a check for six dollars and seventeen **cents.** *Money.*

    f. Sent/scent/cent

        i. I **sent** him a package in the mail. *Verb, to send.*

        ii. The K9 picked up the suspect's **scent** and was quickly on his trail. *Smell.*

        iii. I don't owe you a **cent**. *Money again.*

    g. Waist/waste

        i. Put the belt around your **waist**. *Body part.*

        ii. Don't **waste** energy. *Misuse.*

    h. Weight/wait

        i. If you go on a diet, you may lose **weight**. *Poundage.*

        ii. If you don't get there early, there will be a two-hour **wait**. *Time spent expecting.*

    i. Threw/through

        i. I **threw** the ball as far as I could. *Past tense of throw.*

        ii. It went **through** Mrs. Nonini's front window. *Passage.*

    j. Plane/plain

        i. You fly in a **plane**. *An airplane.*

        ii. We built the water feature along the same **plane**. *Flat or level surface.*

        iii. Speak in a **plain** manner. *Simple, straightforward.*

        iv. The American Indian used to roam the **plains**. *The prairie.*

    k. Hole/whole

        i. The ball I threw through Mrs. Nonini's window made a **hole**. *Something a rabbit might go down.*

        ii. I can't believe I ate the **whole** thing! *Entire.*

COMPLETE

A COMPLETE report is critical to report writing. If an officer omits facts or actions he took, this can have considerable consequences. Investigators may be unaware of potential leads. Criminal cases may fail in court. The officer may find himself at risk if he is accused of wrongdoing and he failed to include important information in the report.

An incomplete report is, quite simply, unprofessional and dangerous.

THE BALLAD OF WOODY

"If it isn't in the report, it didn't happen."

This is a well-known police maxim with regard to report writing. I first heard it in the fall of 1993 when then PFC (now a retired detective) William "Jerry" Wood stood in front of my basic law enforcement academy class and uttered it. After he said it, he looked around the room at us, letting the words sink in. I'm sure we all had blank stares gazing back at him, or some of us may have pretended to understand what he meant and nodded knowingly. But like most recruits, we didn't have a clue.

Years and years later, I found myself assigned to the investigative unit as a sergeant.[1] Who was there as one of the detectives in my unit? Detective Wood, of course. And during my time there, he brought me a few poorly written police reports that had been assigned to him for follow-up. Woody apparently didn't believe in the "groan, get a cup of coffee, and take two aspirin" method of coping. He came to his sergeant instead.[2] What do you think was one of the most common pitfalls that the responding officers had fallen into? Leaving something out of the report. The information wasn't there.

And if it isn't in the report, it didn't happen.

But what does that mean, exactly?

Clearly, whether something happened or not isn't dependent upon whether someone wrote it down.[3] So what does this saying express?

It means that the police report is supposed to include all relevant facts. That is the assumption of the person reading the report. I think everyone

1 I loved being a detective. But I got promoted to sergeant after only two years as an investigator. So when I went back to the investigative division as a sergeant, I made sure my title on my business cards read "Detective Sergeant Scalise." Hey, don't make fun. We all get our joy from different places.

2 Which, in all fairness, is exactly what he should do.

3 If a person wrote a report in a forest and no one. . . . oh, never mind.

Everyone reading your report is counting on it to be complete—including Woody.

will agree that this is a reasonable assumption. Further, the only knowledge many readers will have of the event is based upon what is included in the report. If you don't include it, the reader won't be aware of it.

A report is supposed to include all relevant facts. Ergo, if the fact wasn't in the report, it must not be relevant—this will be the interpretation of those reading your report.

As a particular police academy instructor on this topic once brayed, "The person reading your report isn't a mind reader. That person can only know what he reads."

YOU COMPLETE ME

What is a complete report?

A complete report is one that includes *all* relevant facts.

Notice that this isn't a handy-dandy mathematical equation? It'd be nice if it was, huh? Instead, it is a judgment call. Just like with the issue of being concise, the writer must draw upon knowledge, experience, and common sense to know which facts are relevant and which are not.

In younger officers, this knowledge and experience aren't as deep.[4] Thus, many reports from younger officers are longer than those by

---

4   Hopefully the common sense is there, at least.

veteran officers. Interestingly enough, they still tend to leave out relevant facts at times. This is simply a matter of experience. They aren't sure what is relevant and what isn't.

As I mentioned before, if you reach a point where you are struggling between whether or not to include a fact, it is best to err on the side of caution. There is considerably less potential damage in being a little less concise in favor of completeness than the reverse.

Am I saying one pillar is more important than the other? Is CONCISE the weak sister of the report-writing pillars?

Pretty much, yeah.

Look at it this way. If you put too much in, what's the damage? A cluttered report. An unprofessional report. A report that the detective will have a wonderful time wading through. That's not a good thing. But if you have an incomplete report, what is the potential damage?

Huge.

A lead may not get followed up.

A criminal case might not be made.

Some citizen's civil case that relied on your report may fall apart.

Heck, it could be your civil case, with you needing those complete details to defend yourself. That'd be a bad day, wouldn't it?

Relevant information includes (and often begins with) what the dispatcher or another party gives you while you are enroute to a call. Example? Well, what if the initial call an officer receives is an armed robbery at a liquor store? And while on the way to the location where the robber reportedly fled, the officer receives an update that the robber was armed with a knife. If that officer then encounters the robber, would it be reasonable for him to do so with his pistol drawn? Or his TASER? Or, at the least, to have an impact weapon at the ready?

Certainly.

If that robber was uncooperative with verbal commands, then charged at the officer and fought, what would be his reasonable response? Obviously, physical means would be necessary at this point. Perhaps the robber is badly injured or even killed in the subsequent struggle.

Now flash-forward several days. As the investigation unfolds, detectives discover that the man reporting a robbery wasn't actually robbed. Instead, as it turns out, he thought the suspect "might" rob him and that the suspect was "acting weird" and "may have a knife or something" in his pockets because he was reaching into them. But in his excited state, talking with the police dispatcher, he misspoke his own suspicions as fact.

Given that information, the "robber" just went from a felon to a suspicious person. Would an officer approach a suspicious person who was "acting weird" a little differently than an armed robber who just took money at knifepoint? Sure, there would still be caution involved but perhaps not the immediate display of force.

Move the investigation forward a little more, and the detectives discover that the suspect was mentally ill and not taking his medication. His particular illness causes him to react violently to any perceived threat. Detectives conclude that the immediate show of force by the patrol officer upon contact may have been perceived as a threat by the suspect, who then reacted violently.

So the question becomes, Did the officer do anything wrong?

Of course, in a case like this, there will be investigations at the local level and even perhaps the federal level. The newspaper and other media will render their always astute and unbiased opinion.[5] And there may well be a civil suit against the officer on behalf of the suspect. But that doesn't answer the question. Did the officer do anything wrong?

No.

Not a thing.

He walked into a situation with the knowledge he had and took proper precautions. How could he have known the suspect wasn't a robber? He only knew what he was told enroute to the call. And an armed robber is considered a very dangerous felon. How could he have known the man was mentally ill? He couldn't. And he certainly couldn't have known the nature of his disability and how he would react to both his safety and arrest measures.

If he had known everything up-front—that he was a mentally ill person likely to react violently to a show of force and that he hadn't committed a crime but was behaving suspiciously—he might have responded differently. But the officer didn't know that.

What did he know and when did he know it?

Do you think it might be important to document in this report *exactly* what he knew and when he knew it? Especially because it is

---

5 I imagine that you're picking up on my subtle sarcasm here, even without emoticons.

pivotal to the tactical choices he made? And especially because those choices were entirely appropriate for the perceived situation?

The answer, of course, is yes. If you get an important fact relayed to you while responding to a call, make sure it ends up in your report. Furthermore, make sure that it is recorded in the appropriate place in the chronology of events. It may not play as large a role in the course of events as it does in our hypothetical situation above, but it matters.

This can also come up in self-initiated activities. Let's say an officer is driving along on patrol and sees a white female with a red sweater standing on the corner. So he stops and talks to her. He discovers she has a warrant and arrests her. After arresting her for the warrant, he finds drugs on her, so she gets charged for that, too. Later on, she files a complaint, saying he had no right and no reason to stop and talk to her. What's more, she alleges that he has harassed her on several other occasions. Internal Affairs gets involved. What did we already establish back in chapter one ("Who Reads This Stuff?") would be the number one stop for an IA investigator when investigating a case like this?

The report.

Always the report.

So the investigator reads the officer's report. Though there is obviously nothing in there that confirms what the woman is complaining about, there isn't anything that really contradicts it, either. So there's no help there.

Oh, wait. Did I mention that the officer had received a complaint from a grocer up the street the day before about a white female in a red sweater that was obviously engaging in prostitution? Or that the same grocer asked if the officer could look into it because it was affecting his business?

It would have behooved the officer to have put that fact in his report, don't you think? Granted, a thorough investigation into this complaint would turn up the grocer's request to the officer. The officer himself would certainly mention it to the IA investigator when interviewed. The grocer would confirm it. All's well that ends well, I suppose. But how much quicker and smoother would things have gone if the officer had just included it in his initial report? And, setting aside self-preservation, isn't it an important fact that should be included, anyway?

Any time you have information from Dispatch, from roll call briefings, intelligence flyers, other officers, or personal contacts that impacts actions you decide to take on your own, this information and its source should be cited in your report. What's more, make sure it is goes in the correct place chronologically—right at the beginning, justifying the contact.

Your justification in stopping someone will almost always come into play later on in court, *especially* if it involves drugs or drug use. Ensuring that you have adequately documented your justification in your original report adds credibility not only to your justification but to everything else you did from that point forward.

Looking at it in another way, what if you were accused of some misdeed on one of the calls you handle, like in the above examples, even though you did the right thing? Now imagine that although the "right thing" was done, it was not recorded in the police report. When the complainant brings a lawsuit, you can bet he'll be saying that "right thing" was *not* done. And you can also bet that if his lawyer can "prove" it wasn't, his client will likely prevail.

What could be the result if your accuser prevails or has a case that looks like it may prevail? For starters, maybe the agency will defend you and maybe it won't. It depends on a number of legal issues that I won't go into here.[6] But you could potentially lose your job, or at least a large sum of money. At the least, if the case is lost, your agency could be forced to pay out some money. And these amounts are never small. Then there'd likely be some adjustment to policy and almost certainly some department-wide training held in your honor. That's always a nice little reputation enhancement.

With all that at stake, do you think that remembering that the "right thing" *was* done but just *wasn't* included in the police report might appear a little self-serving at this juncture? Can you see where it might seem just a little to con*veeeeeeen*ient?

It will tend to look that way, even to an objective person.

All relevant facts *must* go into your report.

---

6   The law is a tricky thing, isn't it?

THE REASON FOR THE BOX

There are several ways to make sure your report is complete.

The first way is to make sure you complete all forms. If there is a police form associated with your narrative, fill in every applicable box. The boxes are there for a reason. Someone wants to know that information or the box wouldn't be there. If you have the information, fill it in. If you know the box is on the form, ask the question of your interviewee.

The criminal justice field relies on intelligence and data. You never know which innocuous detail might be of extreme importance to another investigator. It never fails to amaze me, though, how some officers will leave boxes blank out of sheer laziness. If you don't have the information, that's one thing. Maybe it was never available in the first place. If the information was available but you failed to get it, that's another thing entirely. Not good. Learn to ask the right questions. *All* of them. But what if you've got the information in your little notebook or rattling around inside your head and you don't take the time to put it in a box on the form of the report you have to fill out anyway?

That's just flat-out lazy. And I have about zero tolerance for laziness. You should, too.

Photo courtesy of M. J. Rose Images.

Filling out every applicable box is an important element of a complete report.

How important are small pieces of information in those little boxes? Critical.

Crit. I. Cal.

Let me give you an example.

In Spokane, Washington, in the late 1990s, a serial killer was at work. He targeted prostitutes, murdering them in horrible ways. Despite a mounting death toll, he managed to elude police for several years. Law enforcement in the area created a task force dedicated to identifying him and stopping him. Some segments of the community[7] threw in, as well.

I was a patrol officer when this was happening. Doug was, too, and pretty new at the time. Like all patrol officers, we were encouraged to contact prostitutes and johns and to write field interview reports (FIs). Most of us did. I know I contacted a lot of prostitutes during that time period. I wrote a lot of FIs, as well as a number of incident reports. Some of those reports involved assaults and rapes that I don't think the victims would have reported if it weren't for the rapport I'd built with them over time and the fact that there was a serial killer on the loose.

Eventually, investigators developed information about a potential suspect. They believed he may have been driving a white Corvette. These investigators pored over reports and FIs from that time period looking for instances of a male in a white Corvette who was seen or contacted in a particular region of the city or with a prostitute. They found two reports with that information, written by two different patrol officers.

Those FIs provided a catalyst. From that point, the investigation moved more quickly as lead after lead developed. The investigators found that particular Corvette, which had since been sold. They found evidence from one of the victims still inside the vehicle.

That is what you call a major break in the case, boys and girls.

After detectives had a suspect to focus on, they were able to develop more evidence. The killer was captured soon after that. He was later convicted.

---

7   There was some talk at the time about whether the community was apathetic toward the situation because the victims were prostitutes that were, for the most part, also drug addicts. I don't know if that is entirely true, but I do know that the *investigators* in this case certainly didn't feel that way about the victims. They worked tirelessly to find the sicko. And they eventually did.

Now, in case you're thinking I'm about to toot my own horn (or Doug's), I'm not. The two officers who wrote those crucial FIs were Corey Turman and Jason "Chachi" Reynolds. Corey has gone on to become a detective (and a damn fine one at that—I had the pleasure of working with him briefly during my stint as a detective sergeant there). Jason was promoted to sergeant in 2006. The television program *Dateline* came to Spokane and did a story about the two of them.

Neither officer, when each filled in those boxes, had any idea that the information would later become so important. It was just one FI of the dozen or more they'd do that week. And that's the point. You never do know. So fill in *every* box, *every* time.

This doesn't just apply to FIs or incident reports. Some agencies (or units within agencies) focus primarily on traffic enforcement. These officers tend to investigate a lot of collisions. Collision forms, just like every other kind of report form, need to be filled out completely.

WHADDAYA SEE, WHADDAYA HEAR?

Completeness means that you include all relevant observations that you made on a call. Was a subject dressed strangely for the weather? A long wool coat in the summertime might be relevant.

Sweating in the cold? Breathing heavily? Maybe he just finished running from somewhere to where you came into contact with him.

Even more basic, what did he look like? Most of this information will probably be covered by those boxes that you *will* fill out.[8] But something might be worth mentioning in the narrative. A scar or a tattoo. An accent. Something unique.

What evidence did you see? This one is always going to be relevant, as well as very likely a critical point.

These are just a few examples.

All relevant statements must be included in a complete report. What statements were made to you or did you overhear? We're talking about relevant statements here, not every single word. Remember to paraphrase. Include everyone you spoke to and what they told you. Another aspect of

---

8 Right? Huh? Right?

this relates to something we discussed in the chapter about clarity—that is, be clear as to exactly who said which statement.

In some cases, you may want to include negative interviews. What's that? Is it where someone is mean or rude to you during the interview, giving you a negative vibe?

No.

Here's an example. Let's say you contacted two potential witnesses who were in a position to see an incident that occurred. However, both stated they neither saw nor heard anything. Include that. For one thing, this may save detectives time conducting unnecessary follow-up. Moreover, it is also helpful if witnesses change their minds later.[9]

Is this negative interview (or negative statement) something you're going to do on a regular basis? Probably not. We've all got enough to worry about with what *did* happen that we don't have the time or inclination to write down things that *didn't* happen. But in some high-profile cases, this might be important.

YOU DO, BAD GUY DO

Every relevant action *you* took should be in your report. An irrelevant fact such as closing the door to the patrol car when you arrived isn't necessary, unless it somehow becomes relevant to the case. But do not omit any action that is important, or your report is incomplete.

What is relevant? Anything you did that pertains directly to the case.

Ah, there it is. I'm asking you to use judgment, experience, and common sense again. Sorry about that. But you might as well get used to it. That's the job.

Try this, though. If you're wavering on whether a fact is relevant, ask yourself if a person reading the report would find it important. Would that person be lost without it?

Sounds like sort of a "Duh" statement, doesn't it? But you'd be surprised. It works. The reason it works is because it forces you to be more objective about the report you're writing. It reminds you that you are writing a report that will be read by someone with no knowledge of the event other than what you record. So give the "Duh method" a try.

---

9 Which, of course, *never* happens.

It might get you through until the judgment and experience catch up to your common sense.

An important legal aspect of completeness involves including the elements of the crime.

If you are investigating a criminal matter and developing a case to arrest a suspect, you must include all of the facts that support the elements of the crime. Elements of a crime are those facts that must be in evidence in order to arrest someone for that crime.

You'll learn all of this in criminal law class, but let's do a for instance. In Washington State, a person commits a burglary when he:

a. Unlawfully enters or remains

b. in a building

c. with the intent to commit a crime therein.

All three elements must be met for the crime of burglary to occur. If your report includes all the facts that show the suspect had entered a building but you failed to include the facts that showed his intent to commit the crime inside the building, the charge would fail.

What kind of facts might make a difference? Well, if all you found inside was a guy wrapped up in a sleeping bag, would you have a burglary? The man's intent was simply to be there and to sleep. See, with only *a* and *b* above, the charge would be trespassing instead of burglary. If, on the other hand, you found stereo components stacked next to the door, then it would be pretty clear that the man's intent was to commit a crime—theft.

How big a deal is that? I mean, a crime is a crime, right? Sort of. Trespassing is only a misdemeanor. Burglary is a felony. What's the difference? A misdemeanor can get you up to a year in the local jail. A felony can send you to prison (a burglary like this can get you up to 10 years in my state). Big difference.

You can see why it is crucial to be complete and cover all of the elements of the crime that has occurred.

THINK JOURNALISM

After all the slings and arrows I've hurled at journalists, now I'm going to steal from them. Call me a hypocrite. I don't care. Where the concept of COMPLETE is concerned, Journalism 101 has it nailed.

Anyone out there ever write for the school newspaper? Anyone? Oh, sure, no hands are going up. You all learned from the good speller/bad speller exercise, didn't you? Well, I know you're out there. You're the same ones who got my Star Trek reference earlier.

All right, then. For the rest of you. . . .

Excluding entertainment and editorials, journalism is supposed to be a discipline that is fact-driven. For this reason, journalism students are taught early on to make sure that each story or article contains the "FIVE Ws and the H."

The FIVE Ws are *who, what, when, where,* and *why.*

The H is *how.*

The operating theory here is that if you are sure to include the answer to each of these questions in your article, it will be complete. A reader should not finish the article and still have one of these questions unanswered.

Does this apply to police reports? Of course it does. If anything, a police report must be even more fact-based than a newspaper story. After all, the police have been imbued with the power and responsibility to investigate crime.

Let's take a look at how each of these simple questions can be answered in a situation of a minor domestic dispute.

Who did ***what***?

`Lucy broke the vase, which belonged to Ricky.`

Photo courtesy of M. J. Rose Images.

Follow the journalism model for completeness.

The first clause answers the question, Who did what? The second clause provides more complete information. Is it relevant? Absolutely. Would it be a crime if Lucy broke her own vase? No.

When?

```
At 1410 hrs, Lucy broke the vase, which belonged
to Ricky.
```

Now we know when this occurred. But our sentence is getting a little messier. It might work better like this:

```
At 1410 hrs, Lucy broke Ricky's vase.
```

The important issue here, though, is being complete. Here, we have included the *who*, *what*, and *when* of this dispute.

Where?

```
This occurred at 1425 East 91st Street.
```

Slam dunk. So then, *How?*

```
Lucy picked up the vase and threw it onto the
ground, shattering it.
```

This description is clear and concise. Of course, in a real report, the officer will have to detail how he knows this information. Did he see it happen? Did Ricky report it? Did Lucy admit it? Did he see all of the broken pieces on the floor?

On the craft side of the house, notice the use of the verb "shatter" instead of something more mundane like "break." What do you see when I say the word "shatter"? A lot of breakage, right? Now, if a vase cracked into two or three pieces, instead of being spread out all over the living room floor, would you use the same verb? No. You'd say "breaking it into three pieces" or something along these lines. That is giving a complete description. The word choice also speaks to accuracy, which we'll cover in the next chapter.

In the criminal justice field, the *how* of any crime is going to be closely examined. The other pressing question to most investigators might sometimes be *who*, if the suspect is unknown (or denies involvement). But ultimately, the *how* of the crime is of paramount importance.

How doesn't just refer to the crime. It refers to how you performed your job. For example, how was it that you were inside the residence? Did you have permission? A search warrant? Were you in hot pursuit? How did you interview the victim? The suspect? How did you collect the evidence?

For investigative and legal purposes, readers of a police report will focus on the issue of *how*. This is frequently where officers may unintentionally omit information that is important. Be complete as a whole but especially on the issue of *how* something occurred.

Why?

This is the most likely point of the investigation to be unknown. From a legal standpoint, *why* isn't a necessary element in most crimes. Yes, you may have to show what someone's intent was, but you don't have to answer *why* he did it.

For example, if the suspect raises a clenched fist in the air and tells the victim, "I'm going to beat you to death," that easily satisfies the legal issue of intent. You don't need to know, show, or prove that the reason why he wanted to beat the victim to death was because the victim was having an affair with the suspect's wife. The law doesn't always care about the entirety of the answer to "why?"

As an aside, then, is *why* important? It can be. At times, it is important to the investigator when formulating interview strategies. It also seems to be of paramount importance to juries, in my experience.

A word of caution in answering this question—you may report the opinions of witnesses, but always ask them to clarify.

> `Ricky said he thought Lucy broke the vase because she was jealous of his mother. I asked him why he thought this. He said that right before breaking the vase, Lucy said, "You love your mother more than me!"`

Pretty solid take on the *why* in this case, huh?

Any opinion that you offer on *why* (or any matter) must be qualified, but we'll discuss that in the chapter about accuracy. Traditionalists, sharpen your knives now.

ANOTHER TRIP TO THE HOSPITAL

Let's take a look at our earlier paragraph from the lesson about concise reports. The end product was:

> `I responded to Sacred Heart Medical Center. Upon arrival, I contacted Nurse Baker in the emergency room. She advised me that John Trapper was in room 16. Trapper had a warrant. Nurse Baker`

`advised that Trapper had also assaulted Nurse`
`Margaret Burns. I contacted Trapper in room`
`16. I ordered him to turn away from me and to put`
`his hands on his head. He did. I handcuffed`
`him and took him to jail.`

All in all, a concise report. But is it complete? Not really.

What information is missing? A considerable amount, but there are some pieces of information that it is reasonable to assume would be available to the officer. Let's examine those.

`I responded to Sacred Heart Medical Center.`

Let's run this sentence through the 5 Ws and the H for completeness. Remember, relevance is important here, too.

Who? Answer: *I.*

What? Answer: *responded.* This is good, but responded to do what?

When? Answer: Ah, it doesn't say.

Where? Answer: *to the hospital.*

How? Answer: It is assumed that the officer was using his normal mode of patrol, most likely a car.

Why? Answer: It isn't clear, though it becomes so later in the report. It's always good to include such information in the first sentence.

Thus, a more complete opening sentence or sentences might read:

`On August 12th, 2012, at 0120 hrs, I responded`
`to Sacred Heart Medical Center. Emergency Room`
`Nurse Baker reported that John Trapper had a`
`warrant and had assaulted another nurse.`

This puts the reader directly in the middle of the situation with all of his questions answered.

We could continue through the entire report with this exercise, but you get the point. Still, let's look at what else is missing from this report.

`Nurse Baker advised that Trapper had also`
`assaulted Nurse Margaret Burns.`

The officer should obviously investigate this assault. What kind of assault occurred? Was Nurse Burns injured? What kind of injury? Who saw the assault? When did it happen? How did it happen?

Further, *how* involves the officer's investigation itself. How did he conduct the investigation? Whom did he speak to? What did they say? What did he personally observe? What actions did he take? What evidence did he collect?[10]

All of these questions would leap off the page at any police supervisor who reviewed this report—and rightfully so.

How about the remainder of the report?

> **I contacted Trapper in room 16. I ordered him to turn away from me and to put his hands on his head. He did. I handcuffed him and took him to jail.**

Is this enough? It could be. If the officer has completed his investigation and nothing is left except the arrest, this might suffice. Most agencies have certain arrest and transport protocols that should be noted, however.

Could this be considered incomplete, though? Depending on the investigation, yes. While Trapper was compliant, did he say anything? Did he resist the handcuffing process? One would assume not because nothing is mentioned, but the question remains.

Of greater importance, what was Trapper's appearance? Did he have any injuries? Make any statements? Why was he in the hospital to begin with, and who cleared him for release?

As you can see, it is easy to ask a slew of questions about an incident. Your goal as a criminal justice writer should be to leave your reader with no questions that should have been answered in your report.

THE WEIGHT

A police report is often considered the "bible" of an event. This means that third parties (civilians and other criminal justice personnel) will consider it as the ultimate authority for what occurred. Why? Quite a few reasons.

For one, the police are objective in examining an incident.

Two, police officers are trained observers.

---

10 Evidence would consist of statements, photographs of the injury, and medical records, for example.

Three, police officers are trained to include all relevant facts in a police report.

Your report must do the same. Completeness is absolutely critical to a quality police report.

All right. Three pillars down. One to go.

Photo courtesy of M. J. Rose Images.

EXERCISES

1. Choose a recent news event or personal experience. Write a short report about the event. While keeping the report as concise as possible, make sure it is complete. Go through the report and label the 5 Ws and the H. If any are missing, ask yourself why? Revise the report to include that element. (*Note:* If you have large swaths of writing that don't answer one of the 5 Ws and the H, this may be where you can cut.)

2. Review the report you wrote in chapters two and three (movie or *COPS* episode) and see if it is complete. See if you can rewrite it to make sure it is more complete.

3. Crime and Evidence in Action

   a. Access the Crime and Evidence in Action CD.

   b. Log in as yourself. Select the burglary case again. This time, select phase two (investigations).

   c. Conduct the investigation, taking careful notes.

   d. Complete a report based upon your investigation. Focus especially upon the element of COMPLETENESS in your report.

   e. **To access the example of this report, log in to <u>www.cengagebrain</u> <u>.com</u> and access the website that accompanies this book.** Compare your report to the example report.

4. Cengage Learning Criminal Justice Media Library

   a. Access "Reality Check Video—Forfeiture" under Fundamentals of Criminal Justice.

   b. View the video.

   c. Write a short essay concerning why it is important for your report to be complete, based upon what you saw in this video. For example, how might your complete report help with the seizure of assets belonging to a drug dealer you arrest? How can you help a probation officer by writing a complete report? How important is it to be complete if you took action facing the MP-5 replica shown in this segment?

5. Revise your working copy of the example burglary report from chapters two and three to be more complete. Save your copy—we'll be using it again!

6. Are you completely sick of spelling yet? Here's another chunk of commonly misspelled words. Study them and quiz yourself, because you'll see them again.

accelerated	cord	occurring	prejudice	studying
acquire	corporal	official	prepare	succeed
adjourned	corpse	omitted	restaurant	suicide
affiant	excessive	opportunity	robbery	surprise
affidavit	initial	particular	scene	surveillance

among	juvenile	pedestrian	separate	suspicion
arguing	legal	performance	sergeant	testimony
assault	marriage	personnel	sheriff	their
believe	monotonous	possible	similar	thieves
benefited	occurred	precede	staff	vague

7. Confusing Words. These are just a few words that are often confused in police reports with regard to meaning. Just like the spelling words, study these and quiz yourself, because you'll be dealing with these words throughout your career. The word is in **bold**. The sentence should put the word into meaningful context for you. Additional context is in *italics*.

   a. Mere/mirror

      i. I sold my 1970 Nova for a **mere** $500. *Only, minimal.*

      ii. Look in the **mirror** to see your reflection. *Don't spend too much time admiring yourself.*

   b. Steal/steel

      i. Thieves **steal**. *To take.*

      ii. After a theft, the thief must **steal** away into the night. *To sneak.*

      iii. The murder weapon was a stainless **steel** knife. *The forged metal.*

   c. Right/rite/write

      i. You were **right**—it was the butler who did it. *To be correct.*

      ii. You can't do that—I know my **rights**! *As in the Bill of Rights. Something one is entitled to as a matter of law.*

      iii. Prepare for the magical **rite**. *A ceremony.*

      iv. **Write** a good report! *To put words together on paper—or in cyberspace.*

   d. Piece/peace

      i. Happy Birthday! Have a **piece** of cake. *A single item, or a single part of something.*

      ii. In order to know justice, we must know **peace**. *Opposite of war. Quiet.*

   e. Lose/loose

      i. If you don't testify completely, we will **lose** the case. *Not win.*

      ii. Don't **lose** your pen—you'll need it to write reports later! *To misplace, to be unable to find.*

      iii. I dug around in the couch and found some **loose** change. *Scattered, not gathered or bound.*

      iv. They set the K9 **loose** to apprehend the suspect. *Untethered, free.*

  f. Vile/vial

      i. He was a **vile** person. *Despicable.*

      ii. She emptied the medicine **vial**. *Small container.*

  g. Pale/pail

      i. She looked very **pale** and shaken. *White, colorless.*

      ii. I don't have a bucket, but I have a **pail**. *Yeah, it's a bucket.*

  h. Gate/gait

      i. Open the **gate**! *Outer door.*

      ii. He walked with a steady **gait**. *Stride.*

  i. For/four/fore

      i. I work **for** the police department. *Preposition, indicating service.*

      ii. I've been there **four** years. *Number.*

      iii. **Fore**! *Forward.*

  j. Illicit/elicit

      i. He was caught with **illicit** goods. *Illegal, stolen.*

      ii. I was able to **elicit** a confession. *Coax out.*

  k. Counsel/council

      i. Sometimes they call him a lawyer, other times **counsel.** *An attorney, one who gives advice.*

      ii. The city **council** met on Monday. *Group of leaders, representatives.*

CHAPTER 5

ACCURATE

Photo courtesy of M. J. Rose Images.

If you were to ask a civilian which of the four pillars was the most important, a majority would most likely answer ACCURACY. Perhaps the greatest expectation that all readers have of a professional in the criminal justice field is that her report is accurate.

As we discussed in previous lessons, a plethora of different people rely on the police report for a variety of reasons. Therefore, it is absolutely imperative that a report be accurate.

The fact is, writing accurately is the hallmark of a professional criminal justice writer.

Not only that, but inaccuracy is unforgivable. A report that is unclear, wordy, or incomplete is wholly unprofessional, but an inaccurate report is absolutely unforgivable. Every police officer must strive to be absolutely accurate in all reports. This is what it means to be professional.

HOW IMPORTANT IS IT TO BE ACCURATE?

I've already said it once, but it bears repeating: *It is absolutely essential that a police report be accurate.*

If CONCISE is the one pillar where you can cheat a little and your report will still survive, ACCURATE is the pillar that gives you no leeway at all. It is the least forgiving pillar of report writing. Every other pillar has some reprieve—but not so in a failure involving accuracy. Let's compare the consequences.

CLEAR. An unclear report will confuse the reader, but that confusion may cause the reader to ask a question to clarify the matter.

CONCISE. A report that is not concise may be tedious to read. It may muddy the waters. It is definitely a sign of an unprofessional report, but it is unlikely to be a matter upon which a severe misunderstanding may turn.

COMPLETE. An incomplete report raises questions. A reader may wrongly assume that some missing piece of information didn't happen. However, if it isn't mentioned, there may well be enough doubt for the reader to ask the question.

ACCURATE. An inaccurate report is fatal. The reader will see that the information is there in the report, so he will have no reason to question it. Therefore, the reader will accept that inaccurate information as factual and base further decisions upon it. When the fact that this information is wrong is later discovered, it throws all of the work that officer has done (and perhaps all involved officers) into question.

After having compared the four pillars, hopefully you can see how critical accuracy is in a police report.

THE YIN OF ACCURACY

One part of the definition (let's call it the "Yin") is simply to *get it right*. Make sure that the information you present in your report is absolutely correct to the best of your knowledge. There is no excuse for being inaccurate. Whereas some errors in clarity and conciseness could be considered stylistic writing errors, an inaccuracy in your report is a clear indictment of your professional police work. Accuracy is the proverbial pudding where the proof lies. If your report is inaccurate, it reflects that you failed somehow in your investigation.

Of course, it is always possible that the breakdown came between your investigation and the actual recording of the event in your police report. If that is the case, why did this happen? Do you need to work harder at your report writing skills? Note-taking? Memory? Or is it just laziness?

Whatever the problem is, if you want to be (or remain) in law enforcement, I'd suggest fixing it. Like *yesterday*.

As I mentioned, at its simplest level, the concept of accuracy means to *get the information right*—in other words, to report *correct* information.

One way to do this is to conduct a thorough investigation. Ask questions. Listen to what people say. Watch what they do and how they do it. Examine the physical evidence carefully. Keep track of your own actions. Take notes.[1] In fact, take *good* notes, because memory fades. You may have to take a half-dozen more calls before an opportunity arises to write your reports. All of these actions will not only help you to have accurate information for your report but also ensure a quality investigation.[2]

Of course, this will require you to be able to recognize what crime is taking place or has taken place and investigate appropriately. How are you going to write a clear, concise, complete, and accurate report if you haven't gathered all of the facts and details? The answer is, you will not.

Moving along, be advised that the archenemy of being accurate is *assumption*.

1   Your note-taking will not be the same as everyone else's. You'll develop your own style and system, based on how your memory works. In addition to that, as your career progresses, you'll probably take fewer notes.
2   If your jurisdiction allows it and you think it would be a benefit to you, tape record your interviews to later refresh your memory.

Take accurate notes at the time of the incident.

You have all no doubt seen the chalkboard[3] exercise centering on the word *assume*. Bear with me as I put you through it again. It's that important that you don't assume.

"Don't ASSUME," says the grizzled veteran instructor, scrawling the word on the chalkboard.

The students watch without a word.

"Why?" asks the instructor.

No one answers.

"Because," the instructor says, "if you assume—"

Here he draws a pair of lines between the letters so that the displayed word now looks like this: ASS / U / ME.

"—you make an *ass* out of *you* and *me*," he finishes.

It's an oldie, but a goodie.

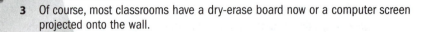

3   Of course, most classrooms have a dry-erase board now or a computer screen projected onto the wall.

Some of you may be shaking your head, thinking to yourself, "I've only heard that about a hundred million times. It is so *cliché*."

You're right. It is cliché. And it became a cliché for a reason. Because it is true.

Do not assume *any* facts that you do not know in *any* investigation. Moreover, you should never report these assumptions as fact. This is sloppy, lazy work at best and, at its worst, can have staggering consequences.

THE YANG OF ACCURACY

The other aspect of accuracy (the "yang," if you will) is being specific rather than general. Pin down descriptions to the most specific level possible.

Be specific in your details. If it is important enough to make note of, it is important enough to be detailed and specific about.

For example, don't just write:

The defendant was driving recklessly.

Instead, describe the specific actions that the defendant took.

The defendant was traveling at 60 miles per hour in a 25-mile-per-hour zone. He swerved repeatedly in his lane of travel, crossing the center line on at least three occasions. He almost hit a parked vehicle in front of 1234 Picadilly Street. Defendant failed to yield at any of the seven uncontrolled intersections he passed, and did not use any of his signaling equipment. During this period of time, between seven and ten pedestrians were walking on the sidewalk.

Although this passage is considerably longer than the single sentence above it, all of the details are important ones. Thus, the report is not only accurate and specific but also complete.[4]

----

4   See how these four pillars sometimes work in concert with one another?

Not only is it important for you to be specific in your own observations and actions, but you must also make everyone you talk to be specific. This includes victims, witnesses, and suspects.

Most victims and witnesses are usually providing information voluntarily, at least at the moment of the interview. All you really have to do is conduct a good interview. Do so with a mind toward what your report will look like. Ask specific questions. If the answer is vague or overly broad, ask follow-up questions to clarify. Make sure you understand *exactly* and *specifically* what the victim or witness statement is. Only then can you record it accurately in your report.

THE ONE-EYED MAN IS KING

We will discuss the importance of eyewitnesses a little later in this chapter, but when it comes to "getting it right" and being specific, I cannot stress how important it is to force your witnesses (and your victim is also a witness) to *be specific*. By doing this, you will accomplish several things. The first, and most obvious, is that you'll have an accurate report.

Yeah, I know. Duh. OK, moving on.

Second, you may have a witness or victim who is lying for some reason about the case (do they lie? We'll cover that in just a moment, too). If that's going on, your specific questions and accurate reflection of the answers will lay a foundation to demonstrate this fact. Certainly, in law enforcement, we don't want to allow ourselves to be manipulated by someone making false accusations.

The third, and most common reason, is because eyewitnesses are not 100 percent accurate. I'm not referring to outright lies here. I'm simply referring to mistakes. Sometimes witnesses will make bad identifications on a suspect. Studies on the issue vary as to how accurate eyewitness identification is, but I think we'll all agree that it is never going to be perfect.

It is tougher yet to base an identification on a description that officers receive from a witness. That's why you have to ask questions that start from the general and drill down to the specific. Male or female, race (or skin tone), height, weight, and clothing are almost always first. Then we roll into specifics that may vary from the perspective of different witnesses (how well did the witness see what the witness is describing and from what vantage point?) or based on the type of suspect. If male, did he have a certain hair style? Facial hair? Something unique in his speech (squeaky voice, a lisp, a cleft palette, use of a particular phrase)?

This doesn't just apply to suspects. This same level of specificity applies to the entire event. What happened, and in what order? We talked about this in our chapter on clarity and completeness, so what is the difference here? Just that you force specificity for the sake of accuracy. Make sure you have the order of events and the exactitude of each event right down the gnat's backside. And you get there by asking good questions and taking good notes.

The point is, *you* as the interviewer (and report writer) have to ask those questions that will make the description of the people and events in this incident as specific—and therefore as *accurate*—as possible.

TODAY'S IS YESTERDAY'S TOMORROW

There is a cynical adage in police work that goes something like this: "Today's victim is yesterday's witness and tomorrow's suspect."

What does this mean? It means that frequently in law enforcement, you will deal with the same people over and over again, though a specific person's role may be different. In one instance, she may be the victim, but two days from now, she might be the suspect.

With an eye toward this little reality, how important does it become to get specific information from this victim or witness while she is only too happy to provide it? Pretty important, because next week you and a partner might be looking for her on a criminal matter in which she's the suspect.

Is that a little too cynical for you? A little too dark? Hey, it is reality and reality is what it is.[5] And I didn't say this applied to *everybody*. But it does apply.

When you interview a suspect, she may be speaking deceptively. Yep, that's right.[6] A suspect may lie to you. Hope you were sitting down before that startling revelation.

5　I've said it in other places and in other ways, but if this isn't a reality you can accept or handle, I'd suggest you consider another career field. Lucky for you, the general writing principles in this book will still apply to most any technical writing.

6　So might a victim or witness, but a suspect usually has more at stake and is more likely to lie.

My guess is, though, that even if you were aware that people lie to the police, you probably don't truly understand how often they do so. Let me clear that up for you.

All the time.

Constantly.

With apologies to The Police,[7] they lie with every breath they take.

There's probably some head shaking going on in the classroom . . . again. A little bit of, "Wow, he's pretty cynical. Probably been a cop too long. Probably a burnout."

If that's what you're thinking, you're right, you're wrong, and you're wrong.

You're right, I am pretty cynical. It is a cynicism well earned. Any cop worth his or her salt develops that cynicism. It is born of experience. It's like getting calluses on your fingertips from playing guitar. It allows you to perform the job. The cops who burn out are the ones who don't control that cynicism. They let it overpower them.

Been a cop too long? Well, not to damage my credibility, but I mostly haven't been a real cop since 2003. That's when I promoted to sergeant and became a supervisor. As a supervisor, you get to do some police work, but mostly you supervise those who do. It's not being a cop all the time, just some of the time. But at least when you're not being a cop, you get to rub up against police work.

Then I became a lieutenant. In that job, I supervised sergeants. I went to a lot of meetings that were vaguely associated with police work. I reviewed a lot of paperwork about police work. I talked a lot about police work, police policy, and police officers. And every once in a while, something major happened requiring a lieutenant to "command" and so I got to rub up against police work again.

At this writing, I'm a captain. Not much "copping" going on in *that* job. It is definitely a leadership role. Of course, I still go to roll calls where police officers congregate for a briefing before shift. They still let me wear the uniform, badge, and gun so that I feel like a real cop. I talk to real cops and wave to them. Occasionally, I manage to catch a whiff of police work as it walks by.

Am I waxing nostalgic for days as a patrol officer? Not really. I still remember the parts that suck, too. I'm just saying that you can't really

---

7   The band, not Five-Oh.

say I've been a cop too long when, in some respects, I really haven't been doing the kind of cop work where people lie all the time for a while now.

A burnout? Negative, Ghost Rider. The pattern is full.

See the previous paragraphs, for starters. Plus, I love law enforcement. I love the honor and intent of those in the field. I've enjoyed the thrills of the ride as I was coming up. I enjoy the opportunity to help improve things now. So I'm far from burned out.

You could write a similar passage about Doug. His career has involved lateral moves rather than promotions, but the progression and development are much the same. Of course, he still slaps the cuffs on bad guys on almost a daily basis, so that trumps pretty much anything I've done.

Anyway, the point is this—if I'm not too cynical (and just a realist), not too long on the job or a burnout, what do you make of my take on how often police officers face lies on any given day on the job?

Ya gotta believe it is true.

People lie all the time. It is unfortunate and dishonorable, but true. When the police get involved in a situation, the stakes usually go up. Sometimes people who don't generally lie will find themselves doing so. These folks are not very good at it and usually recant when confronted. They don't feel comfortable lying,[8] anyway.

But people "in the life"[9] lie as a matter of doing business—*especially* to the police. It is almost like a warped version of a golden rule for them. These people will lie about virtually everything, even when the truth might mean their freedom. Believe me. I've seen it firsthand time after time.

On patrol, and especially on graveyard,[10] I knew when someone was telling a lie. It wasn't hard. If her mouth was moving and sound was coming out, she was probably lying. I always knew when someone was telling the truth, because it felt kind of strange. All my radar instruments spiked and an internal claxon bell rang out. "What's this all about? Oh, I see. This one is actually telling the truth."

---

8 That's how a polygraph works. The mind considers a lie to be a threat. The body responds physiologically to that threat. The polygraph instrument measures that response. This is why sociopaths are sometimes able to defeat polygraph examinations.

9 Meaning professional criminals or people frequently involved in criminal behavior.

10 Where, in addition to the lying epidemic, you'll discover that almost everyone you will encounter is either drunk or high.

Still believe me on the cynical count? It's OK, really. As long as a person is making a joke about it, no matter how dark, macabre, or gallows the humor is, that officer is still OK. She's coping just fine. When the jokes stop, that's when the trouble begins.

So if everyone is lying, how on this green earth are you supposed to write an accurate report with regard to a suspect's statement?

For starters, it's okay if they lie. Really. Just remember this little proverb[11] with regard to suspects: if they're talking, you're winning.

If they're talking, you...are...winning.

Let's say that the suspect is talking to you and she is actually telling the truth. Yeah, I know. We're through the looking glass here, Alice, but stay with me. If she's telling the truth, then you're winning because you've got a truthful statement. Especially if she's confessing to a crime. That's your goal and you just accomplished it.

But what about when she's lying? How can you be winning if she's lying to you?

Because she's talking to you, that's how. Like I said. You know, the proverb?

See, for investigative purposes, it's important to get a precise statement from the suspect if she's actually chosen to be interviewed.[12] A detailed, specific statement that is recorded in a police report will be difficult for a suspect to refute[13] later on, but a vague or ambiguous one is easy to attack. Thus, by locking her into a precise version of events, you have provided yourself or the investigator with a baseline to compare facts against. If the suspect's lie is specific enough, other incontrovertible facts that you discover in your investigation should disprove her statement. That takes care of the jury's reasonable doubt—you've alleviated it by disproving the suspect's cover story. If she later chooses to go to a different story, the inevitable question will be, "Well, this is a new story. This story and the one you told before can't both be true,

11 OK, it's not really a proverb, since I made it up. It's more of a saying, really.

12 Will they talk to you? Many times, yes. It's always worth a shot. Some people are convinced that they can talk their way out of anything. These people deserve the opportunity to try. I figure, if they want to dig a hole for themselves, hand them a shovel. Let 'em talk.

13 Especially if it contains a juicy quote or two. It's hard to refute your own words thrown back up into your face.

so were you lying then or are you lying now?" Either way, she's a liar and her credibility is shot.

The key to all of this is making the suspect be specific. Don't allow her to make vague, imprecise, ambiguous answers. Get specific in your interview and then, by all means, *record those specifics in the police report.*

Another important element to being accurate is to always cite your source. It is assumed in your report that if a source is not being cited, *you* are the source. You saw it, heard it, or did it. So if you are not reporting firsthand information, make sure it is clear to the reader where the information came from.[14]

HOW ABOUT THEM BOXES?

In chapter four when we discussed being COMPLETE, we touched on filling out all of the boxes on any report forms you use, whether it be an arrest report, an informational, a collision report, or just a simple Field Interview. Let's talk now about making sure that when we fill out those boxes, we do so *accurately.*

For starters, spelling a person's name correctly is important. We can hearken back to our chapter on CLEAR and Cachanga Serpaap (pronounced Ke-VIN SMITH), right? There's another reason to be accurate here. As names are put into computer databases, the data are only as good as the information going in. If you aren't accurate with the spelling of a person's name, she may end up with several database aliases in your system. This can be a nightmare for investigators and officers on the street alike. It drives dispatchers nuts who have to run these names because it increases their workload significantly.[15] So be accurate on those names.

The same thing goes for addresses, phone numbers, work addresses and phone numbers, birthdates, height, weight, and eye and hair color—all of a person's horsepower needs to be accurate. Every time you come into contact with someone and make a report as a result of that contact,

---

14 That doesn't mean you have to put an attribution on every sentence or anything like that. Just be clear about whom the information comes from.

15 You might think hitting a few extra keys is no big deal, but when you add it up over the course of a shift, it can be a time killer.

Back to boxes again—be accurate!

you are building a part of your agency's intelligence information. In some larger jurisdictions, that database may only be used by your agency, so any mistakes you make will only affect your fellow officers—not something you want to do!

Even in the case of large jurisdictions, though, smaller neighboring agencies will sometimes query you for information, so your mistakes can filter outside of your own city.

If you happen to live in an area where several agencies share a records database, then a mistake you make will have impact on those other agencies as well. These types of mistakes can cause further mistakes to occur in investigations involving the person about whom you put bad info into the system. If those mistakes are discovered, which they inevitably will be, it could cause some embarrassment for you or your agency, depending on how high profile the case might be. In any event, you're going to have some hard feelings between local agencies (not to mention a negative view by others of you and your agency).

See, *everyone* expects your report to be accurate. All those folks back in the introduction of this book ("Who Reads This Stuff?") are counting on it, in fact. And it isn't at all an unreasonable expectation.

So you might be thinking, "So what if I make a few small mistakes? It's not a big deal." Then let me ask you this. Would you put up with a "few small mistakes" cropping up in your paycheck every two weeks?

No. You count on payroll to be accurate, don't you? And when they're not, there's not a cop around who doesn't trundle down to the payroll clerk's office, pay stub in hand, point out the inaccuracy, and demand (the nice ones just ask) it be fixed.

People have a right to expect the same kind of accuracy from you.

ROLES PEOPLE PLAY

Shakespeare once wrote:

All the world's a stage,
And all the men and women merely players,
They have their exits and entrances,
And one man in his time plays many parts.[16]

Bet you'd never have expected to read Shakespeare in a book about law enforcement report writing, did ya? Oh, well, a little culture never hurt anyone. Much.

Here's the reason for the quote—another consideration regarding accuracy and those boxes you have to fill in on those forms is what *role* a person plays in your report.

When you're entering the biographical data for Cachanga Serpaap, most forms are going to ask you exactly what role he plays in this report. Is he a victim? A complainant or a witness? A suspect? An arrested person? Obviously, this speaks to being clear (see chapter two), but it also dwells in the realm of accuracy. Anyone reading your report needs to have this information clearly and accurately spelled out for them. Most people will have probably read a slew of police reports in the past, so those people will automatically start thinking of each new report in terms of those roles.

For example, if a burglary report comes into a detective, she's going to be thinking of the event against her template of experiences in similar cases. Who's the suspect? Who's the victim and are there any witnesses? When she flips back to the face sheet of your report to find out, she's going to look for that designator that reads "victim," "witness," or "suspect."

---

16 The play this comes from is *As You Like It*.

Likewise, if she comes across a name in the report and it isn't immediately clear what role the person plays, she'll be thumbing back to the part where people are listed and will look for the role designation.

Why aren't we talking about this under CLEAR? Well, we could, I suppose. But the point under accuracy is this: be thoughtful about what role you assign to each person. What did the person do in relationship to the event you are investigating or reporting? If she was a victim, fine. If she also called the complaint in, I don't think I'd list her as "complainant" because "victim" probably trumps that. It's a more accurate description of her role.

Could you have a complainant that is different from your victim? Sure. What if a home was burglarized and a neighbor driving by happened to notice the door standing open. She calls the homeowner (the victim) but gets no answer. So she calls police.

Is she a witness? Yeah, she is. But because all she can report of value was the time that the crime was discovered, she might best be labeled as the complainant.

There's a popular Internet phrase for situations like this—YMMV (Your Mileage May Vary). What it means is that this is just one take on things or one solution. Your agency may have different guidelines (sometimes quite specific) or you may feel like "witness" trumps "complainant." Have at it.

The two role designators that I do think require some caution are "witness" and "suspect." Let's take them in that order.

A witness is generally someone who saw something with regard to the event you're reporting. It shouldn't be used as a catchall for someone who is not a victim or a suspect. If the person didn't observe a piece of the events at hand, then "witness" is probably too strong of a designator.

Some agencies will use "other" as a designator for people like this or "MIR" (Mentioned in Report). It is a good idea to have a specific designator for people who are peripherally involved but not direct witnesses to the event.

Why worry about this? Well, being called a "witness" in a police report is going to result in some shotgun approach subpoenas from both prosecutors and defense attorneys, for one. For another, it is simply a matter of being accurate. If a fight occurred in a bar between the only two patrons, you might have a victim and a suspect, right? Plus, the bartender would possibly be a witness. But how about the bar owner? She's not a witness, even if she shows up while police are on scene investigating. So list her as "other" or "business owner" or whatever designator accurately fits.

"Suspect" is a much more troubling role to slap on someone—unless, of course, it is an accurate one. The word itself has a negative connotation. Make sure that you only attach it to someone who has earned it.

What does that mean? Well, don't call someone a suspect simply because she was identified as one by a victim or a witness. This goes back to forcing people to be specific. If you ask the burglary victim if she suspects anyone and she identifies Johnny Lawbreaker, ask the follow-up question—why?

A good answer might be, "He was casing the house earlier in the week" or "I saw him riding a bike exactly like the one stolen from my garage" or "He's the only one with a key." All of these reasons stack up to a reasonable suspicion. Slap a giant "suspect" role on Johnny in this case.

A not-so-good answer might be, "I just don't trust him" or "He's a crook" or "Everyone knows he does stuff like this" or some other vague, nonspecific reason. In this instance, I'd be hesitant to name ol' Johnny as a suspect. Should he be mentioned in the report? Yeah. I think I'd write something like, "Victim identified Johnny Lawbreaker as a potential suspect but offered no concrete reasons as to why." I might even quote the victim on those reasons.

The thing is, maybe Johnny *did* do it. Maybe the victim's gut is right on this one. I don't want to shut down a potential lane of investigation by omitting it, so we'll put it in the report. But in all fairness to Mr. Lawbreaker, labeling him as a suspect would be inaccurate.

Let's face it—there is a price associated with being listed as a suspect in a police report. If some other officer (or anyone with access, for that matter) runs up someone's name and sees the person listed as a suspect in a burglary, what is going to be the immediate reaction? What if this comes up on a background check for an employer?

What if the suspected crime was assault?

Or child molestation?

"Suspect" is a pretty heavy jacket to hang on someone in our society. So use it wisely. Have a reasonable justification for why that person is listed a suspect.

All that said, you will label men and women as suspects at least as many times as you'll write a traffic ticket in your law enforcement career.

Perhaps more. And you will become a little bit inured to the impact, just like when you write that ticket. Don't stress over it—a lot of crime happens and a lot of people deserve to be labeled as suspects. If they do, call it what it is. Don't be fearful that you'll somehow be sued or something over it. Unless the law changes radically, you'd need to be pretty reckless in this regard for there to be any kind of wrongdoing or damages found against you.

But, at the same time, know *why* you're labeling someone as a suspect. A good rule of thumb is simply to ask yourself if *you* consider the person a suspect. If you do, you do. If you don't, then you probably need to consider a more accurate role to assign to this person.

HOW MUCH FOR THAT DVD PLAYER IN MY LIVING ROOM?

Occasionally, you will be called upon to make a quantitative judgment of some kind. For instance, you may have to accurately estimate the value of an item or the amount of damage that has occurred.

At times like this, use common sense. First off, accept the victim's estimate if it seems reasonable. If it is not reasonable, you may have to conduct some minor research to reach a better conclusion.

Remember that you have a lifetime of experience as well. You didn't come to police work without having lived life, at least a little. Everything you need to know about criminal justice isn't contained in the classes you take at college or what you learn in the academy. You may, and should, draw upon knowledge that is independent of your criminal justice career to make a quantitative judgment. For example, you may have worked in an auto body shop. Thus, you would have a reasonable ballpark estimate of the amount of damage someone has caused to a vehicle. Or perhaps you sold electronics, so you know the approximate value of a stolen television. Maybe you are also coincidentally a stamp collector and know just how much that 1932 Truman three-center is worth. Or maybe you just purchased a lawn mower almost exactly like the one taken in the victim's garage burglary.

When making such judgments, be sure to cite the reason for your expertise. And make certain that you don't fall into using jargon from that particular discipline or former career when you write the report.

THAT'S WHAT PETE SAID

As we talked about in the chapter about the CLEAR pillar, the use of paraphrase and quotations is important in a report. However, these must be done in an accurate fashion.

Remember to paraphrase *accurately*, but quote *exactly*.

A paraphrase must represent the words of the person to whom you are attributing the statement. The words do not need to be exact (by definition, they're not), but the content and the message must be accurate.

A quotation, on the other hand, must be rendered *exactly* as it was made. This is the purpose of a quote—to show the reader exactly what the speaker said. Often, a person's intent, attitude, or regard for the events being investigated can be crystallized well in a direct quote.

What if you wish to quote someone but can't remember exactly what was said? Perhaps you failed to write it down and when it comes time to create the police report, you are unsure of the exact wording.

In this case, you have two options. You may paraphrase, which is the safest response. For example, you might write:

```
Pete expressed that he should be in the hall
of fame.
```

The other option is to qualify the quotation. You may write:

```
Pete said something similar to "I ought to be
in the damn hall of fame."
```

Realistically, it is possible that Pete actually said:

```
"I damn well ought to be in the hall of fame"
```

or

```
"Damned if I shouldn't be in the hall of fame,"
```

but the rendered—and qualified—quotation is fairly accurate. The key is that you've stated the quotation is a qualified one.

Might this statement be challenged by the defense in a court proceeding? Quite possibly. In fact, a judge may even rule against it being admitted as a direct quote.[17] But by qualifying the statement and rendering it

---

17 In which case, you could still testify to the general sentiment.

as accurately as possible, you will not be viewed as having done anything wrong in the eyes of the court.

I'm not recommending this as a method you should employ as a general course of action. The best policy is to quote *exactly*. That's one of the reasons to take good notes. But sometimes you will find yourself in the position I've described, wanting to at least record the sentiment along with a quote that is nearly accurate. That's when this method might be acceptable. If, however, you do not feel that you can render the quotation, qualified or not, with great accuracy, then you must paraphrase.

OPINIONS

What do you suppose my dad said about opinions?

I'll bet you can guess.

If you can't right away, let me tell you a little about my dad. He's a smart man but not much for intellectual bantering. He's worked as a

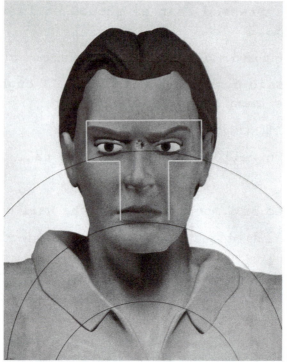

Opinions? I thought we were talking about accuracy!

Photo courtesy of M. J. Rose Images.

welder, but most of his life he's been a meatcutter. He's managed several meat departments for local grocery stores, all of them quite successful. He deals in hard facts and figures and in customer service. He believes in straight talk[18] and honest dealings.

Now what do you figure he came up with about opinions? Actually, when I was younger, I thought he came up with the slightly crude[19] saying (or is it a proverb?), but I later learned how common it is.

Do you know the saying I'm driving at yet? Well, let me just give you the ending of it. Regarding opinions, everyone has one.[20]

We human beings are an opinionated lot. Moreover, we believe highly in the value of our own opinions and in the inherent accuracy of those opinions. We do not tend to be too flexible about them and unfortunately have a stubborn streak when it comes to altering our opinion.

Do police officers have opinions? Oh, yeah. Cops are extremely opinionated. And they're all right. Just ask 'em.

Would you expect any less? Police work, particularly in the patrol arena, is a high-speed, low-drag affair. Most cops are type A.[21] They are the meat eaters of the world. The T. rexes. The warriors. Why? They have to be. They are going out to face bad people.

In one sense, the police are to a municipality what the military is to a nation. The military is a club, not a scalpel. The purpose of the military is simple: to kill people and break things.[22] That's why you shouldn't unleash the military without significant cause to do so—because people will get killed and things broken. That's what the military is for. You don't send them in to deliver food or medicine, either. You can ask them to guard and protect the people delivering the food and medicine, though. Then, if someone else tries to take that food and medicine away, the military will kill those people and break their stuff. Simple.

---

18 Which solves the mystery of where that particular sentiment of mine came from.

19 A father's prerogative is to be a little bit crude at times.

20 If you can't figure it out on your own, ask around. It won't take long for someone to fill in the blank: Opinions are like _____; everyone has one.

21 By type A, I mean driven, outgoing, strong-willed, and aggressive. Type B refers to more laid-back personalities. I realize this is the layperson's usage of these psychological terms.

22 I believe I first heard this description on Rush Limbaugh's radio show in the 1990s, but he may have been quoting someone else.

Law enforcement is a slightly more precise tool than the military. Instead of a club, it is a sword—but still not a scalpel. The job of the police is to prevent crime, but we usually end up responding to it. Patrol, in particular, has a specific function (or should): to answer calls of distress from citizens. To catch bad guys and take them to jail.

For that, you need meat eaters. You need that roaring T. rex. You need warriors. You need men and women who are willing and capable of facing extreme situations that most civilians can't even imagine—and who then emerge victorious.

People like this tend to be a wee bit strong-willed and opinionated.

That's probably one reason why cops from time immemorial have been instructed to *never* put anything remotely resembling an opinion in a police report. I can see this point and, in some ways, agree with it. Generally speaking, a professional police report has no place for opinions. The primary purpose of a police report is to gather and report facts. It isn't a venue for police officers to voice their social, political, or personal opinions, which we've already established are likely to be pretty strong and prevalent.

However, there may be a time when it is appropriate to include your *professional* opinion in a police report.

This concept is not one that would be popular with "old-school" officers who were trained on the "just the facts" method of police work. Once again, we are faced with the fact that we are in a new era of policing and things change. Besides, as you'll see, the "change" really isn't that radical. While I am using the word "opinion," I could just as easily substitute "conclusion."

Still, there are those who would argue that there is no reason to put any sort of conclusion or opinion in a police report. The argument is that the police report is strictly a fact-gathering function. This, however, is a limited viewpoint. Although it is true that the role of the investigator is to gather facts, she must also come to conclusions. These supported conclusions are professional opinions.

Notice the phrase "supported conclusions." Again, the opinions being discussed here are not idle, bar-stool philosophy quips that are shot from the hip. We're not talking about theories or assumptions, either. These opinions are *professional* and *supported*.

So if the term "opinion" is bothering you, go ahead and use the term "professional conclusion" instead. While this may be more palatable, the end result is the same.

FIRST OFF

To include an opinion, you must be careful to avoid any prejudice or stereotype. For example: **"Darnell is black and probably a gang member."**

In this example, if being black is the only "indicator" of gang membership, then this opinion is clearly ridiculous (and actually racist). However, if Darnell is associating with known gang members, has gang tattoos and attire, flashes gang signs, and claims gang membership, then your professional opinion *based on facts* that he is a gang member or associate has merit.

In that instance, though, you would never write something as ludicrous as "Darnell is black and probably a gang member." The level of pigmentation in his skin is considerably far down the list of any consideration for this supported conclusion you have reached, as you'll see below. The tattoos, his own claim of gang membership, and association with known gang members and activities are far more relevant. Other than as a general identifier, the only potentially relevant reason for mentioning Darnell's race might be social or cultural. Because most gangs tend to be racially or ethnically homogeneous (though this tradition is breaking down in some areas of the country, usually out of necessity due to their particular demographics), noting that the suspect shares this trait with the gang members he is associating with is worth pointing out.

It is also important to avoid euphemisms. Though these soft, gentle, and roundabout words may make some people feel more comfortable[23] when discussing a topic or a fact, euphemisms are an unclear form of communication. In many ways, euphemisms are a form of slang and suffer all of the pitfalls of slang: lack of clarity, different regional and social uses, and a short life span. Thus, they have no place in a police report.

---

23 Let me repeat a refrain that you've probably heard once or twice so far in this book. If you're a person who can't comfortably (or at least professionally) deal with people who are vastly different from yourself in any variety of ways, you're probably going into the wrong profession. You'll need to interview victims, witnesses, and suspects who come from different backgrounds, with different careers, different shades of skin color, different religious beliefs, and different sexual preferences, just to graze the surface of the Difference Ocean you will sail on as a cop. If this isn't something you can handle, do everyone (especially yourself) a favor and find another career.

For example, don't write, **"He is living an alternative lifestyle"** or some other euphemism in order to denote that someone is homosexual. Rather, if he is homosexual and that fact is *relevant*, simply state, **"He is homosexual."**

When might sexuality, or even perceived sexuality, be a relevant point in a police report? Well, a hate crime is a perfect example.

The point here is, don't let personal bias seep into your report. Don't let assumptions seep into your report. And don't let weak writing (such as using euphemisms) seep in, either. As previously discussed, all of these are unprofessional. In addition to that, each will color your opinion, if you offer it, as unprofessional, too.

And because the only kind of opinion that should ever be in a police report is a *professional* one consisting of factually supported conclusions, what kind of damage does the appearance of being *un*professional do to that equation?

TEE IT HIGH AND LET IT FLY

If you elect to include an opinion in your report, you must first ask yourself if there is a need for it. Does the report you are writing naturally lead to some sort of conclusion that you should record as a professional investigator? Moreover, did you take certain actions based upon that conclusion? If the latter is true, you most certainly want to explain the

Once you've laid the groundwork, tee off.

Photo courtesy of M. J. Rose Images.

conclusion you reached in order to justify and explain your subsequent actions.

Regardless, when you are about to offer an opinion, you must do three important things:

- Be clear that you are stating an opinion,

- that it is *your* opinion,

- and then list the concrete reasons why you have formed that opinion.

A professional opinion generally works best as a concluding statement. This can be at the conclusion of the entire report or merely at the conclusion of a segment devoted to a particular topic or issue.

Let's look at the following paragraph to illustrate this point.

> ```
> Based upon (1) physical evidence; (2) consis-
> tent statements by three independent witnesses;
> (3) four separate, inconsistent statements made by
> Suspect Hall; and (4) Hall's mannerisms and be-
> havior during questioning, I concluded that Hall
> was being untruthful regarding this incident.
> ```

This paragraph might appear at the end of a report. It might also appear at the end of the section of the report devoted to the Hall interview. Either way, each of the numbered points in this paragraph that support the final conclusion or opinion will have been examined within the report prior to this concluding statement.

To break that down a little further, the reader should know what the physical evidence (number one) is and what it means because the officer has described the evidence. He will have reported how he discovered the evidence, interpreted it, and collected it. Thus, when he refers back to it here, the reader is intimately familiar with the evidence and what it means.

Regarding item number two, the identity and statements of the three independent witnesses must also have been covered earlier in the report. The officer would have described who they were, how he contacted them, and the nature of their statements. Again, the reader is fully aware of these facts already.

What, by the way, is an "independent" witness?

An independent witness is a disinterested party who saw what happened but has little or no stake in the event. Say, for example, someone is standing on the corner of the intersection and sees a collision between two cars. The witness doesn't know the driver of either vehicle. She has no stake in the outcome of the investigation and no reason to be anything other than truthful. This is an independent witness.

Independent witnesses are golden, for exactly the reasons I addressed above. Having three separate, independent witnesses is stellar. What do I mean by "separate"? I mean that not only does each witness have nothing to do with the situation or the people involved in the situation, but neither does each witness have any connection to one another.

For example, if a man, his wife, and adult daughter were all standing on the corner watching the collision occur, you'd have three independent witnesses. None of them know either driver or have any stake in the investigation. However, if your three witnesses were the guy on the corner, a woman in a car stopped for traffic, and a customer in a nearby shop, none of whom know each other, now you have independent *and* separate witnesses to the collision.

Why is this a big deal? Well, consider the odds here. If there is a collision and Driver A says he had the green light and Driver B says he had the green light, now you have a fifty-fifty situation. Who's telling the truth? Hard to say, perhaps. Especially if there isn't anything else to go on. But if the guy on the corner chimes in that he saw Driver B run the red light, that tips the scales. If the guy on the corner, his wife, and adult daughter all say that Driver B ran the light, the scales are tipped even farther.

Driver B, of course, is going to argue that the guy on the corner is wrong. He might even say the guy on the corner is lying. And if the other two witnesses are relatives of the guy on the corner and had the same vantage point, Driver B may say that they're wrong, too, or that the three of them conspired to lie.

Why? Who knows? The whole world must be against him. It couldn't possibly be that he actually blew the light, right?

Compare this situation to having three separate, independent witnesses. How likely is it that three people from three different vantage points all saw the situation wrong? How likely is it that all three saw what appeared to be Driver B failing to stop for the red light when it was actually Driver A? Not terribly likely.

How likely is it that three people from three separate vantage points who have never met each other before all saw Driver A run the red light but then hurriedly conspired with one another to lie to the police about this issue in which they have no stake whatsoever?

Not very.[24]

The key element for you as the report writer is to express how each witness was separate and independent (as well as, of course, describing the vantage point from which they viewed the collision). And in our example regarding Mr. Hall, the police report will have already covered that completely before it is ever referenced in this conclusionary paragraph.

Returning to that paragraph, Hall's four inconsistent statements will have also already been reported in detail. What's an inconsistent statement? It can be as radical as first saying, "I was in Las Vegas at the time" and changing that to, "I was at the house stealing things but I didn't hit anyone." Or it can be more subtle but still inconsistent. Inconsistencies can revolve around the order of events, the time events occurred, the words that were exchanged, or anything else about the case. The key points here are that during these four separate statements, the investigator forced the suspect to be specific (remember that?) and then reported each statement specifically in the report, showing clearly how they were inconsistent with one another. And again, these statements have been described in detail well in advance of this opinion paragraph.

The same is true of the suspect's body language, voice, tone, word choice, and every other behavior that was indicative of deceptive behavior. All of it was documented throughout the description of the interview.

As a result of a good investigation and a quality report about the investigation, when the investigator draws a conclusion in this instance, the conclusion has been *supported by the facts*.

It would not be acceptable to write instead, **"It is my professional opinion that Hall is a liar."** For one thing, this word choice is inflammatory and not professional.[25] For another, though the facts that support

---

24 Of course, we know that some of the witnesses will be wrong some of the time, as explored earlier in the chapter, right? So make sure you get an accurate statement from each witness. Then you (or the investigator who takes on the case after you finish the call) can decide how much weight to put on each of the witness statements, taken in the totality of the circumstances, that is, other statements and especially the physical evidence.

25 One student once asked me if that meant "was being untruthful" is a euphemism. I have to raise my hand and say "guilty" to that. It is a little bit of a euphemism. It is being used in this instance, though, to maintain a professional, detached demeanor. It's not being used to make the reader's landing softer because I as the writer am uncomfortable with conveying the message.

this opinion are in the report, they should be summarized prior to making this conclusion.

MY OPINION ABOUT OPINIONS

If you've been reading carefully, you probably already know my stance on this issue. Although it is a prominent, mainstream mantra that opinions have no place in a police report, I don't entirely agree. Of course, it is all a matter of semantics, isn't it? I say "opinion," you say "professional opinion," and Doug says "conclusion," but we all mean the same thing.

See how important and powerful words are?

My professional opinion on this matter is that it is incumbent upon the investigator to summarize her findings and conclusions in her report, if she should have any. I base this on my years of experience in law enforcement, which included time as an investigator. I say it is all right to put your professional conclusion, based on facts and circumstances you have investigated, into your report.

Just be clear that is what you are presenting—a professional conclusion. Or opinion.

Whatever.

The other thing I think is important to get across is that expressing an opinion in your report is not necessary all the time. In fact, it may not be necessary very often at all. You may only include your conclusion about the investigation in a small minority of your reports. And that's OK. It should only be included when it has relevance. But I am also saying that when it does have some relevance, it is acceptable to include it in your report.

Make sense?

Keep in mind that you will likely come across people who disagree[26] with this sentiment. All I can say is—well, that's their opinion.

TIME TO SUMMARIZE (NOT WINTER-IZE)

When writing an important police report (and which ones *don't* fall into that category?), it is a good idea to consider summarizing or capsulating events at some point in the report. This usually makes sense to do at the

---

26 Sometimes vehemently so.

very beginning of a report or at the very end. Sometimes, though, if you're about to change gears or go considerably deeper into a subject, a summarizing statement might belong anywhere in middle of the report, as well.

If we look back at the "Tee It High and Let It Fly" section of this chapter, we see an example of a summarizing statement. The officer has reached a conclusion and is collecting a concise overview of the reasons for that conclusion. But is this the only time when it makes sense to use a summarizing statement?

No. In fact, you are more likely to find it useful to use summarizing statements to make sense of a long description of events or a justification for an action. As I said previously, you may not offer a professional conclusion within the context of your police reports often—but you will have to explain and justify in just about every report you write!

What does it mean, for the purposes of a summarizing paragraph, to "explain" something? Well, you may have a situation that was confusing or involved. After the call is completed, you'll likely adjourn to a substation or wherever to write the report and describe the events. After four pages of what could be a reality-show version of *Days of Our Lives,* you realize how convoluted the call really was—especially for someone who wasn't there. So, at the end of your report, you do a little summary:

> In summary, Fred Flintstone's daughter Pebbles was engaged in a secret romance with the victim's son, Bam-Bam. When Wilma Flintstone found out about this, she told Fred. Enraged, Fred went next door to assault Bam-Bam. Barney Rubble, Bam-Bam's father, attempted to intervene. He and Fred fought. Barney's wife, Betty Rubble, joined in the fight on her husband's side. Fred struck her in the side of the head with a closed fist. She then struck the giant sundial, causing further injury.
>
> Betty was treated by medics and transported to the hospital, where Doctor Sedimentary diagnosed her with a fractured skull.
>
> I arrested Fred for Second Degree Assault.

This summary leaves out a whole lot. For instance, part of the reason Fred got so mad was not just because of his daughter and Bam-Bam but because Wilma and Barney were involved in an affair last year.

Plus, Barney borrowed Fred's lawn mower a month ago and hasn't returned it yet. Also, Fred had been berated by Mr. Slate at work earlier in the day, so he was in a bad mood. The summary paragraph also doesn't go into the considerable detail that the report itself does with regard to the confrontation and the actual struggle between the parties. The actions of Pebbles and Bam-Bam aren't important enough to make the cut, either.

What you do have is a single paragraph (or so) that effectively summarizes the most important elements of this event. This ties it up in a neat bow for your reader, whether it is a sergeant, the prosecutor, or an administrator.

The reader will love you for this, trust me.

The other thing it does is give you a chance to think over your call one last time. You can reflect as to whether or not you left something out or should cover something in greater depth. In this way, it is almost a precursor to proofreading (which, if you read ahead, is just around the corner).

Another time that you might want to summarize is when you need to justify your actions or a decision. This primarily occurs when you deprive someone of either property or freedom, particularly if you use force to accomplish this.

After writing about all of the facts in a particular situation, it is helpful to the reader (and sometimes to you) to summarize your reasoning for the action you are about to take. For example, if you had to force entry into someone's house or seize a piece of property, stating your justification, including not just facts but the legal basis for this action, is a good idea.

Using force is where this is particularly useful. As you'll learn in other books on criminal law and procedures (as well as liability!), the use of force by police is largely governed by the standard established in *Graham v. Connor*, a Supreme Court ruling. The Court establishes several criteria that it will look at when determining if the officer's use of force was objectively reasonable. A summary paragraph can lay out those applicable elements for the reviewing party, whether it is a supervisor within the agency, a lawyer somehow involved, or a judge if the report has been stipulated to.

Here's an example (remember, we are joining this report in progress):

```
During the struggle, the male threw an elbow or
forearm, hitting me in the mouth.
```

> The male, Beaves, had a confirmed Department
> of Corrections (DOC) warrant. He had not been
> searched and was wearing oversized clothing,
> making it difficult to observe if he was carrying
> any type of weapons. It was apparent he was not
> willing to comply by the way he immediately
> attempted to flee from officers on scene. The
> suspect had elevated from being resistive to as-
> saultive when he delivered an elbow strike to an
> officer.

> At this time, I delivered 2 knee strikes to
> the side of his abdominal area.

This example clearly covers those elements that the courts have said they will consider when examining whether or not the use of force was reasonable. Anyone reading the report for that purpose (or preparing to argue that purpose—e.g., your lawyer in a civil suit) has a convenient paragraph from which to draw the salient points.

Here's another, this time with the use of force being an exceptional driving technique—intentional intervention:

> The suspect had already committed 1st degree
> assault by ramming one police vehicle, and
> I believed that Officer MacLeod was most
> likely injured. The suspect has already shown
> his lack of concern for the safety of officers
> or the general public by his reckless driving
> and ramming of vehicles. It was obvious that
> he would not hesitate to ram into innocent
> civilians or other police officers if he was
> allowed to continue driving. The suspect's at-
> tempt to make a U-turn and avoid spike strips
> showed that he was motivated to continue flee-
> ing officers. I determined that a low-speed or
> stopped blocking maneuver was the safest way
> to prevent the suspect's escape and protect
> the community.

As you can see, this summary paragraph directs the reader's attention to answering those all-important questions about the reasonableness of using a particular level and type of force.

PROOF OF THE CRIME

As a rule, no report is finished until it is proofread.

Why?

Lots of reasons.

Writers make mistakes. Sometimes the mistakes are merely typographical, but even these can be dangerous. Simply leaving out the word "not" in a sentence, thus negating it, can change the entire meaning of the sentence.

```
Jasper was booked into jail.
```

```
Jasper was not booked into jail.
```

Big difference, huh?

Lesser mistakes chip away at the professionalism of the report. They break up the reading flow of the reader as she notices the errors.

The police report is a professional, official document. It should be error-free. Only proofreading ensures that this occurs.

Also, proofreading can make you a better writer.

Are you shaking your head and asking, "Huh? How can that be?"

There are two ways in which this is true.

Proofreading involves a careful and deliberate review of what you have already written, looking for grammatical, spelling, conceptual, and structural errors. If you find them, you fix them. Obviously, this makes you a better writer because your final product is better written.

But by proofreading not only your own work but the work of others as well, you will gain a better understanding of the errors commonly made by writers. You will see what works in narrative and what does not. This will serve to increase your writing skills.

Is there *always* a need for proofreading? The answer, quite simply, is "yes." Even on the rare occasion in which you may dash off a brief report without a single error and include all relevant information, a quick reread in order to double-check the document is necessary.

Errors have a way of happening unexpectedly. Published books and articles sometimes have errors in them.[27] You may even discover

---

27 Trust me on this one. My first published novel had several typos in it that somehow slipped in after my final fixes went to the publisher. My final fixes to the publisher for my second book in 2007 ran 14 pages. And these were fixes, not edits.

errors within this textbook. Proofreading is the best defense against this happening to your report.

HOW DO YOU PROOFREAD?

First, reread the document slowly. Read it word by word. Watch for spelling mistakes or grammatical ones. If this is your greatest weakness, one way to focus solely on this aspect of the report is to read it backward. Begin with the final paragraph first and then move backward paragraph by paragraph. This will remove the "story" content of the report and allow you to pay more attention to spelling and grammar.

However, don't lose sight of content. Does your report make sense? Double-check specific details, such as times or locations, against your notes. Ensure that your chronology is correct. Make sure you used quotation marks where you intended to quote someone. Be aware of any disjointed breaks between paragraphs that may require some sort of a transitional sentence.

Checking for content is best done by reading the report in a normal forward direction. However, imagine that the report isn't yours and you are not familiar with any of the events. That will be the vantage point of the person who reads your report.

Another proofreading method is to read aloud. When you read silently, your brain "helps." In other words, if you left out a word in a sentence, your brain knows what you meant to say, so it helps you out as you read silently by filling in that word. You might read the sentence and skip right over the missed word without the mistake ever registering, because you know what you meant to write.

Reading aloud defeats this tendency. The speech function uses a different part of the brain than reading silently. When you read sentences aloud, a missing word will be glaring. So will a particularly awkward sentence.

Or has this ever happened to you—you're reading along in a book or magazine when some word or phrase sparks a memory of something else? Your mind drifts off, thinking of the memory while your eyes continue reading down the page. Pretty soon you're two paragraphs farther along and have no idea what you've just read. Reading aloud helps stop this from happening.

I know, I know. Who wants to sit in their car or at a computer terminal and read out loud? Everyone else in the area will see you, cock an eyebrow, and say, "Well, hello there, Officer *Crazy*." Right? Maybe so.

I can't argue against that. It could happen. Probably will. But it doesn't change the fact that reading a report out loud is an excellent proofreading method.[28]

Another option in proofreading is simply to have another person read the report. Much in the same way your reading aloud will catch mistakes that your silent read might fill in, the other officer is not familiar with what you have written and will catch those same mistakes when silent reading. This is a particularly effective method if the reviewing officer wasn't even on the call you're writing about. Also, another officer may know something that you don't—proper spelling, for example, or perhaps a fact that is helpful.

Most word-processing programs have spell-check and grammar-check functions built into them. These are excellent proofreading tools, but they don't replace your eye and your knowledge. Furthermore, they are not infallible. Spell-check, as we discussed earlier in this text, may tell you that a word is correct when it is spelled right but is the wrong word or the wrong form of the word in the context you're using it. Besides, anyone can add any word they want to that particular computer's dictionary. If you're working on a community computer of any kind, you run the risk of someone else's misspelling being considered gospel by the program you're in. That is the "garbage in, garbage out" theory at work.

Grammar-check functions are even less reliable than spell-check. If you go through your report and take every suggestion that a grammar-check program throws at you, your report will be nonsense by the time you're finished. The English language is just too tricky. You must have the grammar knowledge in your own head, folks. That's the only way. Then, if the grammar-check program flags something, you can treat it as a situation in which the computer is saying, "Hey, you might want to look at this." But most of the time you're probably going to say, "Uh, no. That's perfectly correct. The squiggly green line is wrong."

English is just too complex. Even though the programmer can fit the rules into a piece of computer software, there are so many intricacies and exceptions that the computer can't be very accurate. In fact, I once read, "Remember, English doesn't borrow from other languages. It follows them into dark alleys, knocks them down, and then rummages through their

---

28 And besides, "sticks and stones," as they say.

pockets for loose grammar!"[29] Don't trust grammar-check functions. Use them as nothing other than a little indicator that you should take a look at something and decide if it needs to be changed or if it is just fine as it is.

Proofreading also gives you an opportunity to revise[30] the report if necessary. In a perfect world, you would have time to plan the report, write a rough draft, revise the report, and finally, proofread it. In reality, most cops plan the report on the fly, write a rough draft, and revise it while proofreading. Many reports don't get changed much at all. This is just the way the world works because of the demand for the officer's time.

You may be fortunate enough to not be so pressed for time. If that's the case, take the methodical approach. If, however, you are in the position most patrol officers find themselves in, you'll have to learn to work quickly. And when you work quickly, there is a greater propensity for mistakes. Therefore, you must proofread. And help your partners out and proof their work, too.

You may not catch every error in every report, but if you develop good proofreading habits, the work product that you do turn in will be of a higher quality and will reflect well upon you.

FINAL ACCURACY

I said it before and I'll say it again—your report must be accurate. Everyone expects that of a police report, and it is not an unreasonable expectation. An inaccurate report can have terrible consequences in some situations, but even day-to-day inaccuracies can sabotage your work and the efforts of others.

Accuracy is the final pillar that must support your police report.

---

29 Kevin O'Shaughnessy.

30 Professional writers, in both fiction and nonfiction, do an incredible amount of revision. In fact, you might say we do more revision than writing. That is part of the craft of writing—the honing and tweaking of the written word. You probably won't have the time to devote that kind of attention to your reports. But at least one close pass over each report will save you tons of trouble down the road. And you'll get better at it as you go, too—if you do it.

EXERCISES

1. The Movie Quote game. Pick your top 10 quotes from movies. Write them down as exactly as possible. Then watch those scenes from the movies and compare your quote word for word with what you hear on screen. You may be surprised at the frequency with which even famous lines are misquoted.

2. Pick a full-page advertisement from a magazine. Spend 60 seconds observing the page. You may then either write down everything you observed as accurately (and completely) as possible OR ask a friend to quiz you and you can write down the answers. Questions should be about specifics: What color were the woman's shoes? Was there a buckle on her purse? Did the man have blue or brown eyes? Which hand rested on the barbeque? These types of details train your mind to think along these lines.

3. Repeat exercise 2 with a different photograph, but allow yourself to take notes. Compare the results. This will also sharpen your ability to take concise notes that still have meaning.

4. Crime and Evidence in Action

   a. Access the Crime and Evidence in Action CD.

   b. Log in as yourself. Select the drug arrest case. Select phase one (patrol officer).

   c. Conduct the investigation, taking careful notes.

   d. Complete a report based upon your investigation. Focus especially upon the element of ACCURACY in your report.

   e. **To access the example of this report, log in to <u>www.cengagebrain</u> <u>.com</u> and access the website that accompanies this book.** Compare your report to the example report.

5. Cengage Learning Criminal Justice Media Library

   a. Review the "Eyewitness Identification" video under Criminal Evidence/Procedure, which discusses the issue of the accuracy of eyewitness identification.

   b. Write a short answer (one paragraph to one page) to this question: What can you do in your initial response and *in your report* to help mitigate this problem?

6. Revise your working copy of the example burglary report from chapters two, three and four to be more accurate.

   a. You may have to deduce or surmise certain facts to make this possible. For the purposes of this exercise, you may do so. But also look for inaccuracies and inconsistencies within the report itself. It may be clear what is accurate and what is not.

   b. When you have finished with your revision for accuracy, go over this example burglary report one last time—proofread! What you should have at this point is a good example of a burglary report instead of the poor example originally provided. Check it against the revised example at the back of this book.

7. Spelling is all about accuracy! Here's a final installment of commonly misspelled words. Study them and quiz yourself, because you'll see them again.

accommodate	define	extortion	prevalent	spontaneous
acquaintance	definition	feasible	probably	staph
adjourned	description	forcible	proceed	tentative
anonymous	dispatched	height	professor	traffic

coming	drunkenness	immediately	prosecute	trespassing
comparative	embarrass	interest	pursue	unnecessary
conscious	emergency	intimidation	receiving	victim
controversial	evidence	investigation	referring	warrant
corpse	existence	larceny	relevant	written
criminal	experience	liable	resistance	youth

8. Confusing Words. These are just a few words that are often confused in police reports with regard to meaning. Just like the spelling words, study these and quiz yourself, because you'll be dealing with these words throughout your career. The word is in **bold**. The sentence should put the word into meaningful context for you. Additional context is in *italics*.

   a. Capital/capitol

      i. The new property room was a **capital** improvement. *Of physical substance.*

      ii. The legislature meets at the state **capitol**. *Government.*

   b. Quiet/quite

      i. Please be **quiet** in the library. *Don't make a sound.*

      ii. I thought I was **quite** clear about noise in the library. *Wholly, completely, positively.*

   c. Presence/presents

      i. Christmas requires the **presence** of Santa Clause. *Being there.*

      ii. He brings **presents**. *Gifts.*

   d. Air/err/heir

      i. You and I both breathe the same **air**. *Oxygen and other gases.*

      ii. To **err** is human, they say. *To make a mistake.*

      iii. He is the only **heir** to the estate named in the will. *The person who will inherit.*

   e. Allowed/aloud

      i. No smoking is **allowed** in the theater. *Permission.*

      ii. I can't believe he spoke her name **aloud**! *Given voice to.*

   f. Bald/balled/bawled

      i. His head was **bald**. *Without hair.*

      ii. He **balled** up the paper and threw it in the trash. *Made into a ball.*

      iii. The child **bawled** about the lost toy. *To cry.*

g. Bare/bear

    i. I could see his **bare** buttocks. *Uncovered.*

    ii. Park rangers warned us about the **bears**. *Yogi or Smokey.*

h. Vise/vice

    i. His grip was like a **vise**. *Tight.*

    ii. Coffee is my only real **vice**. *Bad habit.*

i. Pain/pane

    i. After my collision, I was in considerable **pain**. *Ouch.*

    ii. The burglar broke the window **pane**. *Glass.*

j. Do/due/dew

    i. What can I **do**? *The verb.*

    ii. How much of the loan is **due**? *Time to pay.*

    iii. The grass was covered in **dew**. *Condensation.*

k. Lone/loan

    i. He was a **lone** wolf. *Solo.*

    ii. I paid off my car **loan**. *Money lent.*

CONCLUSION

So now you have the four pillars. You're ready to be turned loose on the criminal justice world, armed with a pen or a word-processing program. Right?

Right?

Wrong.

Well, sort of wrong.

The one component that is left is the one thing Doug and I can't give you.

Practice.

You have to practice. Like any skill, if you want to improve, you have to practice at that specific skill.

Reading helps. If you read a lot, you'll become a better writer. Much in a way that roadwork and bag work help a boxer, reading helps a writer. But in order to get better at writing, you have to write.

I had a karate *sensei* once who was very pragmatic. He worked us hard in the *dojo*, and when we sparred, the punches and kicks were real. Sure, we pulled them a little bit to avoid serious injuries, but they still landed with enough force to cause black eyes, bruises, and so forth. It was realistic training.

My sensei was adamant about not fighting outside of the dojo unless no other choice remained. But he was just as adamant that if you engaged in a fight, you ended it in a quick and resounding fashion.

"Every guy out there thinks he can fight," he told us. "Every guy thinks that skillful fighting is some kind of innate skill that he was issued right along with his Y chromosome. He'll say things like, 'I don't know karate or boxing or anything, but I'm a good fighter. I just go crazy.' But crazy doesn't cut it. Just like any other skill, you have to train to fight to get better at fighting."

Sensei was right. And the same holds true of writing, no matter what kind we're talking about. You have to write to get better at writing. Still, everyone thinks that they're good at it, just like guys do about fighting.[1] For example, almost every time I have a book appearance or go to a party where I don't know most people, at least one person says to me, "Oh, I could write a book. It's easy. You just write stuff down."

---

1 And just like *everyone* thinks about their own driving and lovemaking skills.

I ask him how much writing he does on a daily or weekly basis.

"Oh, not much," the person always says with a smug, dismissive grin. "But I could write a book, no problem. And it'd be a best seller."

I'm certainly not going to crush his dreams,[2] because I believe a person can accomplish just about anything he sets his mind to. But at the same time, writing is a lot like fighting. Or hockey. Or fighting in hockey, for that matter. That is, it is a lot harder than it looks. And you have to practice to get good at it.

Last words on the subject of report writing for the street officer. Ready?

Report writing is a skill, so you gotta practice.

And pay attention to your report writing so that it improves.

Remember the four pillars. Strive to be clear, concise, complete, and accurate.

Remember that the police report is the final representation of your work product. It is how many people will judge you.

Put the effort in—finish the game.

And be safe out there.

Photo courtesy of M. J. Rose Images.

---

2   If it is a dream he's having and not a delusion.

BONUS FEATURES

Ah, you poor people. You thought you were finished with me. Well, you can be, if you want to be. Everything you should know to start busting out some quality reports is in chapters one through six. But if you want some additional information that might help you out, then the bonus features in the following appendices are for you.

APPENDIX A

What Am I Looking For?

Photo courtesy of M. J. Rose Images.

In my career, I've been fortunate to take on a number of different roles. In each of those roles, I was generally looking for something different in the police report. Just to give you an idea what the different consumers of your report are likely to look for, I'll go over each of the roles I've been in during my career and what I was looking for.

Patrol Officer

Quite honestly, when I was a patrol officer, all I cared about when I looked at another patrol officer's report was basic content. Did he cover the portions of the investigation that I expected him to cover? Did he include the interviews he conducted? Did he clarify any points of probable cause that I was relying on?

At the time, I didn't care if the other officer's work had shortcomings, as long as what I needed was in the report. I realize that sounds mercenary, but that's the way of it. I guess I always figured, "I'm not his mother." Or more specifically, "I'm not his sergeant."

His report had one function for me and one function only—to include the information he collected that I needed to support my own report. Everything else was his problem—or his supervisor's.

That said, how do you think it looks to another officer if you hand him a report that only covers a third of what you were supposed to cover (and is, therefore, not complete)? Or what if your report is so unclear that the other officer can't tell what you covered?

It looks bad.

Of course, cops are such a nonjudgmental lot that you probably don't have to be worried about being ripped for the shortcomings of your report.

Yeah. Rii-iight.

Other police officers will judge you on your report.

Field Training Officer

Ah, now the stakes have changed. When I became a field training officer (FTO), I was responsible for the training of a recruit. That included reviewing his reports before they were turned in. So what did I have to look for?

Everything.

Realistically, the FTO is probably going to be the most critical person ever to read your report, at least this side of an attorney. As an FTO, I looked at the reports written by my recruits[1] from every angle. Everything in this textbook came under consideration. Was the penmanship neat? Were all the boxes filled in? Was the grammar correct? Were the words spelled and used correctly? Was the structure of the report chronological? Did it make sense? Was it complete? Accurate? Clear? Concise?

The FTO must look at *everything*, because he is training the recruit. I have to admit, I was hell on my recruits about reports. Some (most? all?) definitely didn't appreciate it at the time. I don't know if they appreciate it now. Probably not. But I know I did the right thing to be hard on them about reports.

A report should not ever get by the FTO with a single error in it. That's a tough standard to meet, but that's the way training should be. This is the period in a police officer's career that is setting the stage for what kind of cop he's going to be. Not only will setting a high standard on reports have the specific result of making him a better report writer, it will set a general standard for his police work overall. **To see an example of a completed FTO report, log in to www.cengagebrain.com and access the website that accompanies this book.**

Detective

I was a detective for two years. I was pretty much the same as every other detective when it came to patrol reports. I'd open up the file and look down at the bottom of the report to see who had written it. That gave me

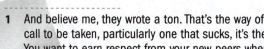

---

1   And believe me, they wrote a ton. That's the way of the world. If there's a report call to be taken, particularly one that sucks, it's the rookie's job to take it. You want to earn respect from your new peers when you're a rookie? Jump on those calls with gusto.

a good idea of what to expect. Sometimes I'd sigh in relief. Other times, I'd groan and make a trip to the coffeepot for a refill and some aspirin.

In reviewing a patrol report as a detective, clarity was a critical point. So was being complete. I wasn't there on the call that the officer was writing about. All I could go on to understand the events was what the officer had written in the report in front of me. If things weren't clear, I was lost. If information was missing, I had to assume it wasn't gathered or that actions weren't taken.

The detective relies heavily on the initial officer's report. I had to make a decision on how to proceed with the case based on the information in the report. Which leads should I follow? Which witnesses should I interview?

I also looked for procedural errors in the report that might hamstring my options. This is where clarity is so important. Miranda warnings, for instance, are a common issue that law enforcement officers deal with. As the detective, I need to know if the suspect was issued Miranda warnings and if so, what his response was to those warnings. Did he understand them? Did he waive his rights and agree to answer questions? If he answered questions, were they pre- or post-Miranda?

The same holds true with the defendant's right to an attorney. In some instances, the particulars regarding that exchange between the officer and suspect dictated whether or not I was allowed to even approach the suspect again for questioning on that subject. I won't try to explain that concept here, but suffice it to say that detectives in our division were actually issued a flowchart covering when they could or couldn't recontact a suspect with regard to his right to an attorney. If it can be that confusing of a legal issue for the investigator, how important do you think it is that the arresting officer writes a clear report when it comes to whether the suspect was advised of his right to an attorney and whether he asked for one or not?

As a detective, I wanted to work every case. I held onto them as long as I could and tried to clear each one with a satisfactory result. I wanted to solve 100 percent of the cases my sergeant gave me, preferably with an arrest.[2]

---

2   Why did we all become cops, anyway? To help people. How? By throwing bad guys in jail.

Even so, as a detective I had to prioritize my caseload. Some cases were fast-breaking, some were front-burner cases, and others were back-burner. I may have even clung onto a couple cases that weren't even on the stove, but I wasn't quite ready to give up on them.

In prioritization, issues like the nature of the crime were certainly at the top of the list. A rape got more attention than a shoplifting, for example. But all things being equal, where do you think I put my efforts first? Or most? Into a report that was confusing and seemed to be missing information? Or into one that was clear and complete?

If the report is your final work product, you want that case to be worked, right? Well, most detectives have some discretion in their caseload. If you want to be the case on the bottom of the detective's stack, write a confusing, incomplete report.

Patrol Sergeant

As a patrol sergeant, I looked at reports in two ways. The first way involved my duty to review and approve reports. In this mode, I read a ton of reports, many at 0400 hours in the morning, through bleary eyes. Sometimes I might have looked like I was agreeing with the report because I was nodding so often, but in reality, I was falling asleep and catching myself. Graveyard can be rough.

A sergeant is looking at your report for content…and more.

The sergeant reviewing and approving reports is looking mostly at content. Is the report clear and complete? Are the actions of the officer spelled out and justified? Are the elements of the crime enumerated? Is the probable cause clearly described? Were policies and procedures followed? These are the primary issues an approving sergeant is looking at.

If a report is particularly horrible or contains something that it shouldn't (sarcastic tone, for example), an approving sergeant might still approve the report but make a copy for the officer's supervisor (if he's not it). Or he might kick the report back to the officer to be fixed.

Either way, the key for the approving sergeant is *content*. If the spelling is horrible or the grammar is poor but still decipherable, that is probably still going to pass muster as long as the content is good.[3]

However, most sergeants who review and approve reports also supervise a number of patrol officers. One of the duties of a sergeant is to review the performance of the patrol officers assigned to him. These reviews might be as often as quarterly or only once a year, but report writing is definitely one of the skills that the sergeant will have to rate the employee for.

So even if a poor report makes it through the approving sergeant due to adequate content, the other shortcomings are going to be noted by the sergeant for reflection in the employee's performance review. That's important, because in some agencies, performance reviews are linked to promotional opportunities or pay.

A sergeant isn't just rating report writing when he reads an officer's report. In fact, he's rating almost everything about the officer when he reads that report. The officer is telling the sergeant what kind of job he is doing by what he includes in the report and how he describes it. By reading this report (and others), the sergeant will get a picture of the officer's self-described performance in such areas as interview and interrogation, application of criminal law and criminal procedures, adherence to policy, investigative logic, and just about anything else the officer describes.

Now, let me ask you this. If your police report is essentially a written report card on your performance that your sergeant will read before writing your performance review, what kind of report card do you want to

---

3　I'll leave it to you to determine whether that is the way things should be or not, but it is the reality in most places. Too many reports to read, too little time to worry about anything beyond content.

present? I mean, you have all of the power and opportunity here to make a favorable impression. Shouldn't you take advantage of it? Especially because writing a good report is—oh, I don't know—your *job*?

Now, in all fairness, I never judged an officer solely on his reports.[4] You have to get out into the field and watch the officers in action. But reports were an indicator, so I looked at them carefully.

Detective Sergeant

It may vary from jurisdiction to jurisdiction, but my brief tenure[5] as a detective sergeant had me reviewing cases with solvability factors and deciding which to assign for follow-up. Given that resources were limited, I could not assign every single case that had solvability. Depending on the ebb and flow of the cases coming in, I might be able to assign between 30 and 60 percent of the cases I looked at.

That means that I had to "file" between 40 and 70 percent of solvable cases that came to my office. What does "file" mean? It is a nice euphemism for reviewing the report and then not assigning it. What happens to that case?

Nothing. It dies on the vine. Nobody follows it up. Nobody works it. The bad guys gets away. Sucks, huh?[6]

With those kinds of choices, what factors do you think I considered in making my decision about which cases were worked and which were filed?

If you're guessing that the quality of the police report was one factor, you're spot on.

There were plenty of other considerations,[7] too, but a clear, complete, concise, and accurate report had a far better chance of being assigned

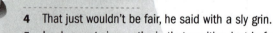

----

4   That just wouldn't be fair, he said with a sly grin.

5   I only spent six months in that position just before I was promoted to lieutenant.

6   Is this acceptable to you as a civilian? I sure hope not. Police staffing levels are sometimes too low to do any better, so you have to prioritize. Still, the citizens of a community deserve the absolute best police service that they choose to afford.

7   What kind of crime it was, how egregious the suspect's actions were, how much evidence there was and the quality of that evidence, who the suspect was—a prolific criminal always got special attention—if there'd been a rash of that kind of crime recently, what the detectives' caseloads were, and so forth.

than a sloppy one. Granted, I would assign a rape arrest over a bicycle theft no matter what the inherent qualities of each report might be. But if the other factors in play were roughly equal, I'd assign the one with the better report.

Why?

Two reasons. One is that a cleaner report will make for an easier investigation by the detective. He won't have to wade through a mess of a patrol report before he even begins his investigation. From my perspective as the supervisor, that is a more efficient use of that resource (the detective's time).

Second, a quality report is an indicator of a quality officer. It is not the sole indicator by any means, but it is *an* indicator. And a quality officer is more likely to have conducted a good investigation that is free of procedural errors. Once again, that makes for a cleaner follow-up investigation by my detective, which is a more efficient use of that resource.

Is it fair to assign one case over another based strictly on the quality of the report? No. And I didn't. But it is fair—and efficient—to give it strong consideration when two cases are similar in other ways.

I'm reminded of a story I read years ago in a book about the writing business. The subject under discussion was the proper formatting of manuscripts and packaging of submissions. The author of the book was trying to impress upon the reader how important it was to follow standard guidelines but also to follow the submission guidelines of whichever agency or publisher you were sending the work to for consideration.

He related the story of a secretary who was tasked with going through résumés that had been submitted for an open position. Her boss was supposed to decide who would get the job, but had procrastinated. Now it was Friday afternoon. He wanted the top five candidates before he left for the day so that he could make his decision over the weekend. Unfortunately for the secretary, there were over 100 applicants.

Sound like an impossible task?[8]

---

8   We all face such *Kobayashi Maru* situations in life. How we solve them tells the world about our character. Oh, and if you don't know what *Kobayashi Maru* means, go rent *Star Trek II: The Wrath of Khan.* You'll be glad you did.

Ever resourceful,[9] she came up with a solution.

The applicants were all given a very specific format in which to address the application. So the first thing she did was go through the stack of 100 and eliminated every single one that did not adhere to that addressing format. As a result, she got down to 70-some applications.

Then she looked to see to whom it was addressed, and she eliminated anyone who sent it to the wrong person, spelled the right person's name incorrectly, or misidentified that person by gender or title. That got her down to into the 50s. Next, she looked at the writing on the front of the envelope. If it wasn't neat, she dumped it. That got her down to somewhere in the teens or low 20s.

Lastly, she opened the remaining envelopes and looked at the résumé inside. If it did not adhere to the format, it went on the garbage pile. That left eight.

She reviewed the final eight for content. From that process, she selected the best five and gave them to her boss on his way out the door.

I imagine that the boss and the secretary had wildly different weekends. The boss, I figure, goofed off all weekend. After going to the lake on Saturday, playing some golf and watching TV on Sunday, he reviewed the five candidates[10] over coffee on Monday morning before he came to work.[11] Then he decided which candidate to hire.

Our erstwhile secretary, meanwhile, gathered up the 95 applications she had rejected and took them home with her. She felt guilty for basing her decision on what she thought might have been unfair criteria. What if one of those discarded applications contained a stellar candidate? So over a glass of wine that evening and the next, she opened every single application and reviewed it carefully.

Know what she found?

Regardless of which criteria (format or penmanship) she had used to reject it, none of the 95 rejected applicants were more qualified than the eight she had actually reviewed in detail.

9 As all employees with lazy, stupid, or procrastinating bosses must be.

10 I was actually surprised he didn't ask her to rank them, too, so that his "decision" would be easier.

11 Rolling in at around 10 hundred hours, I'm sure. Bosses. Sheesh.

True story. *Old* story—back before word processors, even—but still true. Presentation matters and it presages quality.

Patrol Lieutenant

At the level of mid to upper management, I looked at reports in a different light. I didn't read every report that all of the officers under my command wrote. I read the ones concerning incidents that rose to a level that required my attention. What kinds of incidents might these be?

Pursuits.

Collisions.

Any uses of force.[12]

Citizen complaints. **To see examples of a pursuit review, collision review, use-of-force review, and complaint review, log in to** www **.cengagebrain.com and access the website that accompanies this book.**

Are most, if not all, of these situations in which officers might make mistakes? Or even get into trouble? Are they areas for which the agency has some potentially large liability issues?

Yep.

So what was I looking for? I looked for a report that was quite clear, complete, and entirely accurate. If I needed to know a piece of information regarding the incident before I passed it up to my captain, it had better be in the report. In fact, one fact might be the axis upon which the whole situation turns.

What if the fact actually was in play or the action I was looking for actually did occur, but the officer just failed to include it?

Wonderful, but remember what we said about how things can look awfully convenient in situations like this?

Although I might have had the opportunity to interview the officer regarding the report, most of the time I had to base my recommendation on the written report. That recommendation might have concerned whether a use of force was within policy. Or if a collision was preventable. Or if a citizen complaint had any merit to it. Which box I checked and what comments I recorded had a potentially profound impact upon the line officer.

---

12 This could be physical force, the use of a tool such as a TASER or baton or a K9 contact (yes, that is a euphemism for "bite").

You want your lieutenant to make the right decision, don't you?

I do, too.

So write a good report.

Patrol Captain (Division Commander)

As one who commands an entire division, I'm looking at reports in many of the same ways as in previous roles. I do need to review the report in reference to collisions, use-of-force scenarios, pursuits, or citizen complaints. All of these have already been vetted by a sergeant and a lieutenant before they land on my desk, but I still have to take a hard, independent look at them before deciding if the action was justified or if the conduct was proper. In that way, a commander addresses a report in much the same manner as a lieutenant.

More than that, though, I am looking for trends that may be developing. Because I am reading all of the use-of-force reports or pursuit reviews or whatever in the entire division, I'm in the unique position to see

Photo courtesy of M. J. Rose Images.

A division commander may only see 5 percent of your reports but will make important decisions based upon those reports.

if certain trends are developing within the division as a whole. Are officers resorting to a particular tactic sooner than in the past (say, TASER use)? Is that particular technique working well or not? Are we initiating pursuits for low-level misdemeanors and continuing said pursuits further than we should be? These are the kinds of things that influence whether or not I implement (or recommend to the chief) a change in policy.

Did I say policy?

Yes, I did.

What does that mean to you if you're the line officer with boots on the ground, pushing a cruiser? Well, policy pretty much dictates what you can do and how you can do it. Policy is to a law enforcement agency what the rule book is to a sport.[13] You want your policy to be reasonable and not unreasonably restrictive.

If I see an event or a trend based on the reports that have come through the chain of command, I am duty bound to consider if those events should have an impact on policy. Should I adjust the policy as a result of these behaviors? If so, how? I can tell you this; in my career, I have rarely seen a policy adjustment become broader in scope. Most changes, not unlike court decisions, tend to be more restrictive in nature.

If I'm contemplating this sort of change, I'm going to review the reports for background. Not the administrative reports, which I will have already read, but the officer's actual report of the incident. Hopefully, what I discover is a reasonable officer making reasonable decisions (often in an unreasonable situation not of her own making). If I'm concerned about some trend, I can review the specific events in each of the individual cases to see if there is a common thread.

If the reports are all well-written, detailed reports that adhere to the four pillars, I'm going to have the answers I need. I will know what the situation was, what the officers chose to do, and why the officers chose to do it. I may even know that they considered and rejected other options.

Armed with this knowledge, I can make the right decision regarding policy. Maybe reading those reports convinced me that we were looking at a statistical anomaly in which individual events just happened to cause this trend, but that policy should remain. Or I might decide that the officers and the agency need to be protected and the policy changed.

---

13 An imperfect analogy, because the LAW is also like the rule book.

Either decision has an impact on *every* officer and supervisor in the division, not just the ones involved in those past events.

Another consideration as a division commander is more on the human side of things. As a command officer focusing on those "command-y" things we focus on, you will slowly lose touch with the experience of the line officer. Ironically, you need this touchstone to keep making the right decisions on behalf of that officer. A good report can help a little in that regard.

As time passes, a command-level boss will have less direct interaction with the newer members of the agency. There may come a time (depending on the size of your agency, it could be *now*) when the only way in which that captain knows an officer is by a name on a printed page. That may be a roster or deployment list or something like that. It may be on a report that comes through the chain. Do you think that the captain will start to form an opinion of that officer based on the quality of his reports? Of course he will. At that stage of the game, what else does he have to go on?

Command-level officers are not going to read any more than a small percentage of the total reports generated by your agency. They are going to read the ones that involve something sticky—a crash, a use of force, a citizen complaint. They will probably account for no more than about 5 percent or so. But because you never know which 5 percent of your reports are going to get that particular set of eyes, shouldn't you write all of your reports in a manner that would satisfy even the most critical commander?

Believe me, it is a much nicer experience to learn after the fact that the captain reviewed your report on a particular matter than it is to have him show up in person looking for an explanation.

Et Cetera

There are, as we discussed early in this text, any number of other people who are going to look at your reports. In that earlier section, I discussed some of what those people in those roles might be looking for. I haven't been in any of those particular roles, so I won't rehash that here. I think—or at least I hope—that you're getting the picture.

Your report may be scrutinized by dozens or even hundreds of people.

What do you want them to see?

What do you want them to think about you?

Photo courtesy of M. J. Rose Images.

DISCUSSION POINTS

1. With so many different people just in the law enforcement arena having different needs regarding your report, do you believe it is practical to do a sufficiently good job on each report to satisfy everyone? Or should you decide which ones are more important and focus on those?

2. How does knowing the different perspectives your separate audiences may have on your report affect how you write it?

3. Which of the roles covered in Appendix A are likely to see the majority of your reports? Why?

4. Which of the roles are likely to see the fewest? Why?

5. As a general rule, the higher rank a person holds, the weightier the issues he deals with on a daily basis. If one of your reports reaches a department head, what can you safely assume about that incident? What expectation should that department head have of your report?

6. Now that you have read this book (to include an appendix and these discussion points—wow! I'm impressed), how would you rank the importance of this skill among the other skills in your field? Has that ranking changed at all since before you read this book? Why or why not?

APPENDIX B

Looking Ahead

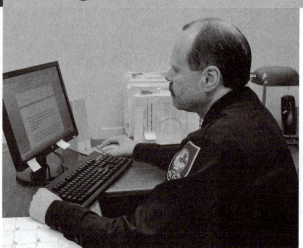

Photo courtesy of M. J. Rose Images.

Keep on Writin' in the Free World

Technical writing in the law enforcement arena doesn't end with police reports. There are any number of other documents you may find yourself writing in this career field. Though the emphasis of this book is on report writing, I want to touch on some of these other types of documents you might have to create.

Why should you care? Because as a line officer, a well-written memorandum may be what helps get you selected for the SWAT team. It may be what results in you attending some excellent and exciting training you want to receive. As an investigator, a letter might garner information that solves a case you're working. Or if you're a hiring/background investigator, a well-written letter may result in getting the information you need to round out an applicant's file.

As a supervisor, a commendation you write will have an impact on the officer receiving it. So will her performance review. And so will your written review of any incident, such as a pursuit or a use of force.

Just like in your police reports, good technical writing will help you in other parts of your career. Written communication is an important skill to master. It doesn't end with the police report.

Professional Letters

At some point in your criminal justice career, you may have to write a professional letter. This could take on any variety of forms. In my own police career, I have written letters of recommendation for prospective law enforcement applicants, letters to other agencies requesting assistance in their jurisdiction, and letters to citizens requesting information or explaining police actions.

As you can see, the specific purpose of each correspondence may be different. However, the purpose of any and all professional correspondences is consistently the same—to convey information in a professional manner.

It is important to remember that the recipient of your letter may know nothing about you or your agency. This recipient may well judge you specifically and your agency in general based on your letter. This is why it is important to be professional.

A professional letter generally follows a strict format. The address and other contact information of the sender are listed first, usually indented flush to the center of the page. The remainder of the letter is flush left to the margin. A letter is single-spaced but double-spaced between paragraphs. That last part sound familiar?

Always include the date of your letter, followed by the full name and address of the recipient.

Following the addressee information, you may elect to include a line announcing what the letter is regarding. For example:

`Re: Case #07-123456`

After all of this "header" information, begin the letter with a salutation. For example: *Dear Officer Kopriva* or *Dear Chief Wiggum*. If you are unsure who the specific recipient should be, you may address the person strictly by title, as in *Dear Investigative Sergeant*. Follow this salutation with a comma or a colon, as you prefer.

After the headings and the salutation, you begin the body of your letter. This should be written in a professional manner. Exercise the same writing skills discussed throughout this course. Make certain that your letter is clear, complete, concise, and accurate. Proofread the document just as you would a police report.

Begin your letter by immediately addressing the reason for writing it. The following example is one way to do this:

> **The purpose of this letter is to inform you that your case has been set for trial on May 1, 2012.**

Once you have stated the purpose of the letter, proceed with any explanation or clarification necessary. In the above example, you might cover what courtroom the trial will take place in, who the judge will be, and what time it begins and ends each day.

Conclude the body of your letter with any directions or requests you might have. In the example, you may direct the recipient to meet the detective and the prosecutor to review testimony or when to come to the courtroom in order to testify.

Once you have achieved the goal of your letter and conveyed all of the necessary information, close the letter in a professional manner. The most recognized way to do this is to use the word *Sincerely*. Other terms, such as *Warmest Regards* or *Yours Truly* do not have the same professional detachment and could be misconstrued.

After your closing, space down four lines and type your full title and name. Once the letter is printed out, you then sign the letter above your typed name.

Before sending your letter, always proofread it a final time. Sometimes you catch things on paper that you missed on the computer screen. Remember, you are sending an official document, representing yourself and your agency. Professionalism is a must. **To see an example of a professional letter, log in to www.cengagebrain.com and access the website that accompanies this book.**

Memoranda and Proposals

In any law enforcement agency, a great deal of communication occurs via memoranda. This is true for a variety of reasons. Law enforcement agencies are open "24/7," meaning that employees work around the clock. It is not always feasible to get all decision makers together at one time because of shift work. It is also not always possible to put out information to all employees at one time in person. Thus, the memorandum (memo) was born.

Memos also provide a written record of decisions and directives. Members can all reference the memo directly, thus minimizing the inevitable "message drift" that can occur when information travels from person to person orally.

You know what I mean. It is the telephone game all over again. Everyone leaves their own stamp of interpretation on a piece of information when they pass it along. They add a little speculation, perhaps, and maybe they leave out something they see as inconsequential. The end result is not a uniform message. Conversely, the message of a written memo doesn't change from reading to reading.

The purpose of an internal memo is much the same as a professional letter—to convey information. However, the memo is an internal document, designed for the specific audience of that particular agency. This includes both commissioned officers and noncommissioned support staff such as records personnel, dispatchers, and clerical staff.

A memo may be used to disseminate any type of relevant information—a policy change, an event announcement, or a particular directive. The memo may be directed at the entire agency, a specific unit within the agency, or even to a single person.

A memo may originate from the chief of police, a line member, or anywhere in between.

What all memos have in common, however, is that they should be professional documents intended to convey information. As such, you should always remember that most internal documents in public sector agencies are discoverable by the public at large, including newspapers. In addition to writing with a purpose, always write as if everyone in the community might read your memo—because they just might.[16]

A formal memo has a heading that generally contains four items: to whom it is addressed, from whom it originated, the date, and the subject matter.

This information is usually in bold print in order to be extraordinarily clear. In some instances, the information presented in a memo may be classified. If you happen upon a memo that does not include you somehow in the *To:* line, it may be advisable not to read it. To put it more

---

16 All it takes is for someone to fill out a Freedom of Information Act request and your memo can be splashed on the front page of the local newspaper.

generally, if it ain't for you, it ain't for you. Direct your inquisitive little eyes elsewhere. Some agencies stamp the security level of the memo on the document so that there is no doubt.

A header in a memorandum may look like this:

```
To:      Officer Stefan Kopriva

From:    Chief William Wallace

Date:    May 5, 1995

Re:      Amy Dugger Case
```

Just as in a professional letter, the body of your memo should begin by stating the purpose of the document. Be clear and direct. Because you are writing for an internal audience, it is generally acceptable to use more jargon and abbreviations than you would in a police report or a letter.

Once you've stated the purpose of your memo, the remainder of the document is dedicated to conveying the intended information. This may involve a number of possible pieces of information. For example, you may wish to disseminate information or request to attend training. Regardless, the body of your report must contain the facts that are important for your reader.

How should you format the memo? The body should be single-spaced, with double spaces between paragraphs. The text should be flush left to the margin. Write in complete sentences, just as you would in a police report.

How long should the memorandum be? The answer is the same as with a police report. It should be as long as necessary in order to be clear, complete, and accurate—and no longer.

Does any of that sound familiar?

It is always a good idea to end the memo with a concluding statement or request. For example:

```
I request that Detective Tower attend the
upcoming training in Homicide Investigation.
```

or:

```
Officers will refrain from parking in the red
zone next to the building.
```

Generally, there is no need to close a memorandum like you would a letter, because the header clearly states who originated the memo.

Remember, your memo is an official document. Be professional. **To see an example of a memorandum, log in to <u>www.cengagebrain.com</u> and access the website that accompanies this book.**

Commendations

Agency morale is a nebulous concept to grasp. Frequently, much of what affects morale is simply communication. As a general rule, the better an agency communicates vertically and laterally, the higher the agency morale will be.

Another thing that affects morale is recognition for doing an excellent job. All too frequently, police officers, corrections officers, probation officers, and other criminal justice professionals do exemplary work that too few people hear about. On the flip side, you know that any time that a law enforcement professional makes a mistake, *everyone* will hear about it.

Much of the time, the work these individuals do from day to day is worthy of recognition. On occasion, an employee does something that rises above that already high standard. In instances like this, the employee should

Photo courtesy of M. J. Rose Images.

Formal commendations have a positive impact on morale.

be commended. Often, it is the employee's supervisor who writes a commendation letter for this purpose. However, nothing precludes one employee from writing a letter of this nature to recognize the actions of a peer.

Hear that? It means that you don't have to wait until you're a sergeant to write a commendation letter for one of your fellow cops.

I recently reviewed a commendation letter written by a 17-year veteran commending the work of his sergeant. The sergeant has been on less than 10 years and has been a sergeant less than two years. However, the veteran officer was so impressed with the day-to-day leadership and decision making of this young sergeant that he sent a letter of commendation up the chain of command. The catalyst for his letter was a particular incident, but he noted that the sergeant exhibited this same high performance level on a daily basis.

Was this officer just being a sycophant? Not a chance. He's not looking for a promotion. He's already on the SWAT team. He intends to complete his career as a patrol officer. So he has nothing to gain by "sucking up." On top of all that, he is a man of considerable talent and integrity.

No, the commendation was entirely genuine. And it was written by a subordinate about his supervisor, a rare event. More often, it goes the other direction. Either way, the world would be a better place, wouldn't it, if people took the time to say "Nice job" once in a while?

In addition to recognizing exemplary performance, a written commendation also serves as a record of the event. This can be part of the officer's personnel file, as well as a keepsake for that officer.

A commendation letter can be in standard letter format or it can be in memo format. Some agencies have a standard or a preference on this matter. In either event, simply adhere to those formatting conventions that we have previously discussed.

As in a letter or a memo, begin your commendation letter with a stated purpose. An example of this might be:

`I am writing this letter to commend Officer`
`Chisolm for his actions on September 1, 1994.`

Once you've stated the purpose of your commendation, you must set the stage for the reader. As in your police reports, assume that the reader knows nothing of the events that you are referring to. It isn't necessary to include every detail as you would in a police report, but you should include the facts that are relevant to the actions you are commending.

This way it will be clear to the reader why the employee should be commended.

If the letter is recommending a particular award, then you must justify why the award should be given. Make sure to meet all of the criteria for that award. In essence, your letter is pleading your case to the decision maker.

A commendation letter should be only as long as is necessary to clearly, completely, and accurately relay the events or actions that are being commended.[17] Remember that commendation letters are often read aloud when presented to employees. So imagine an assembled group standing while the letter is being read. A three-page commendation letter in most instances would be too long. People will begin to lose concentration after a while. They'll shuffle their feet, cough, and let their attention drift. And if there are kids in the audience, three pages is probably about two and a half pages longer than they'll be able to sit still or be quiet for. Being concise and using powerful language help avoid this.

At the same time, you should avoid hyperbole or exaggeration in your commendation letter. If the performance is worthy of commendation, then no exaggeration should be necessary. Besides, exaggeration is really just another form of lying. If the action of the employee was an exemplary one, simply stating the facts as they exist should make that point clear. Don't cheapen it by overstating it. Also, don't assume emotions or thoughts on the part of the employee or anyone else involved in the incident. Just state the facts.

As with other professional documents, when you have completed the goal of the commendation letter by conveying all of the information you intended to, you must close.

Your closing should include whatever action you recommend be taken. Writing something like **Officer Chisolm should be commended for his actions** is sufficient. If you are recommending the officer for an award such as Employee of the Month or for an official decoration such as a Silver Star, state so in your closing. In that case, you may wish to close with a single sentence after stating the award recommendation.

If you choose a letter format for you commendation, the final part of the letter will be your title, name, and signature.

---

17 Sound familiar? I'm like a broken record on those four pillars, huh? Or, to keep up with the times, maybe I should say that I'm like a iPod on Shuffle and Repeat.

While I think good work should always be recognized and commended, don't be out there writing commendation letters like they're free for the taking. Make sure the reason for the commendation is worthy. If you give out commendations and awards at the drop of a hat, the commendation or award is devalued. But don't be stingy, either.

And write a good one. **To see an example of a commendation, log in to www.cengagebrain.com and access the website that accompanies this book.**

Performance Reviews

Most large companies, including police agencies, have some kind of performance review process. The process usually includes written documentation of the employee's performance. When you become a supervisor, that responsibility usually includes some kind of performance review for your subordinates.

Your first responsibility is to be accurate, of course. Whatever the rating system, the employee should be fairly graded. Don't allow your personal likes ("halo effect") or dislikes ("pitchfork effect") for the employee influence your objective rating[18] of that employee's performance.

Most performance reviews are not nearly as in-depth as something like an FTO report, which examines in-depth every action the officer took during that rating period. But you should have some general observations about the employee, as well as some specific instances that support those observations and the related scores.

As a general rule, the farther away from "average" that you get in your ratings, the more you'll need to write to justify that rating. This is true whether you've given an employee an extraordinarily high or extremely low rating. Such a deviation requires explanation. Make sure that the narrative you provide to justify that rating matches the rating you've given. In other words, if you gave the employee a "9" on a scale of 1 to 10, but your description actually describes a performance that merits a "4," you've got a problem. Either the rating or the narrative is wrong.

18 Sad news, but when you become a leader, you effectively give up the luxury of being subjective in this way. You must be *objective* as a leader. Anything else and the troops will sense it and will lose respect for you and your judgment. That doesn't mean you can't like or dislike someone. It just means you have to be fair with her and to her, whether you like that person or not.

Not only is the performance review a formal document, but it becomes a part of most employees' permanent personnel file. If an employee later has performance issues or is involved in a critical incident, her performance reviews for the last several years may be examined closely by other supervisors, investigators, the media, or anyone else remotely associated with the critical incident. Therefore, you should write in a formal voice and make a professional presentation. **To see an example of a performance review, log in to www.cengagebrain.com and access the website that accompanies this book.**

Formal Reviews

As a supervisor or administrator, you may have to review a use of force, collision, or pursuit at some time. Though the format varies from agency to agency, most of these reviews only require a brief comment from you before forwarding them to the next level of command. Therefore, once you have read the packet thoroughly, you should summarize your review succinctly. Your skill at being concise but complete will be on display here.

These reviews may or may not be confidential, internal documents, but it is a strong possibility that the event you are reviewing may be one that the community you serve is concerned about. Will your review itself be reviewed?

White Papers

Call it what you will ("position paper" is another word I've heard used), a white paper is essentially an analysis of a particular subject. You might be examining the interaction between your agency and the jail and contemplating other alternatives. You might be exploring whether your detective position should be a rank or a position. Should we drive Fords or Chevys? What should the goals of this agency be? What will some new program be like?

This kind of document is most like an essay, a college paper, or a nonfiction manuscript. It will need to be clear, concise, complete, and accurate because it is presenting a scenario and offering conclusions. You may be trying to convince a chief or even a mayor to follow your direction. A poorly written paper in this situation could have a major impact on the direction of your agency. (For example, do we build a new police station or buy an existing building?)

Luckily, you will probably have more time to write this type of document than almost any other kind. Take your time. Revise. Seek outside review, if possible. Put the best possible face you can on this white paper, because it not only will reflect upon you but will have a significant impact on whether your idea or position is followed or not. **To see an example of** **a white paper, log in to www.cengagebrain.com and access the website that accompanies this book.**

E-Mail

Let's talk about something more mundane. Most agencies utilize e-mail extensively. Even though e-mail is informal in a personal setting, I would strongly recommend that you lean heavily toward the formal side of this equation in the business world. For one thing, it is difficult to detect tone in e-mails (hence, the huge growth in the use of emoticons). You don't want to be misunderstood in the workplace.

For another thing, all e-mails are still official documents. They are open to public disclosure. For that reason, you should remain at least quasi-formal and abstain from using any questionable language or profanity. Certainly don't forward jokes or other objectionable material.

E-mail in the workplace is a great way for people to communicate across the 24 hours of shift coverage, particularly if people are also on rotating shifts with different days off. But it can also be fraught with land mines, as I alluded to earlier.

Treat e-mail the same way you would treat a public bulletin board. If you wouldn't pin the note up on the board for the recipient (and the entire world) to see, don't hit SEND.

Also, be careful with hitting REPLY ALL when you meant to hit REPLY. If you do that, everyone who received the original e-mail will also receive your reply. Not only does this cause unneeded e-mails to clog other people's inboxes, it might also be embarrassing if your comment was flippant.

Of course, we're not going to send any like that, anyway. Right?

Riii—iight.

This is where I shake my head and mumble to myself about how "They listen but then when the time comes. . . ."

Trust me, though. You'll only get burned once in an e-mail mistake. And then you'll believe me.

Et Cetera

I'm certain there is a plethora of other formal documents you'll be exposed to or have to write. I won't go into any others here. No matter what the format is or whether it is formal, semiformal, or informal, if you apply the technical writing skills that you use in report writing, you'll be in good shape.

Final Thoughts

So here we are again. At the end. Bet you're glad. Let me leave you with just a couple of things to file away.

Law enforcement is a job that requires (and needs!) honorable men and women. If that fits you, welcome aboard. If it doesn't fit you, go away. Now. If you're dishonorable, you're just a lawsuit and a scandal waiting to happen.

Although you will *earn* the opportunity to be in law enforcement by taking tests and demonstrating common sense, physical prowess, and good judgment, please also always remember that it is an *honor* to serve. It is an honor to wear that badge on your chest. So wear it honorably.

The one thing that can't be stressed enough is how important your police report is to the entire agency, your victims, and the population as a whole. If police officers don't take the time to make sure that they write clear, concise, complete, and accurate reports **every time**, we are not doing the job we are paid to do. The number of bad guys we arrest or the quantity of drugs we get off the street won't matter if we can't get convictions based on our documentation.

Both Doug and I have a lot of experience in teaching and helping others with their report writing skills. We have taught recruits at the academy level and in the field, college students, and some veteran officers who just need a reminder on its importance. Please take the information in this book to heart. All jokes and banter aside, we believe what we say and practice what we preach. I hope this book has helped you and that you have a long and successful career.

Remember: Write reports like people's lives depend on it. Because, in one fashion or another, they really do.

See ya on the streets.

Photo courtesy of M. J. Rose Images.

EXERCISES

You may not feel entirely comfortable with each of these exercises, but give them a try. Practice doesn't make perfect, but it does make better.

1. Write a professional letter.

   a. You are a detective requesting personnel information on a suspect named Jon Dough, who used to work at AnonImus Locksmiths. You are investigating him for burglary. In addition to his work history, you would like to know about his particular job skills and performance.

2. Write a proposal.

   a. Your department currently works eight-hour shifts. Select a different shift configuration. Describe how it works, why it is better than "straight eights," and convince the reader (your department head) to make this change.

3. Write a commendation.

   a. You are a sergeant. One of your officers responded to a fire for traffic control. The fire department was not yet on scene. She heard sounds from inside the fully involved house. She ran in and rescued a small child. Describe the event, why it merits a commendation, and what that commendation should be (you can make up the commendation itself, but make sure to include the criteria and how your officer meets it).

4. Write a performance review.

   a. Write a performance review for the absolute best you've ever performed on a job (or a sports team). Include your strengths, weaknesses, and specific actions during the rating period.

   b. Do the same, only for a time when you've performed poorly.

5. Write a formal review.

   a. Find an incident in your local media. Review the archived news stories and especially any of the reports or findings that were issued publicly. Summarize the event and draw a conclusion in an objective fashion.

6. Write a white paper.

   a. Present a radical new concept that represents a major change to your department head. Outline the reason for the change, how it will work, what the benefits are, and how you will transition. Make sure to include the obstacles that exist and how you will overcome or mitigate those obstacles.

7. Write an e-mail.

   a. You just found out you have to work overtime on Saturday at a community event involving safety and kids. You don't want to because you planned on playing softball. Send an e-mail on the subject to:

      i. Your best friend on the department, who is the player/ manager of the softball team.

      ii. Your sergeant in an attempt to change her mind about your assignment.

      iii. The community leader who heads the program you'll be working at on Saturday (assuming you didn't convince the sergeant to change the assignment).

      iv. Your department head, briefing what occurred at this event.

   b. Are these e-mails different in tone? Why or why not?

   c. Should they be? Why or why not?

APPENDIX C

A Final Review

For those of you who are gluttons for punishment, here is a final review of the lessons in this book. Fill in the blanks. Check Appendix D to see how you did.

Good luck.

Introduction

1. Report writing is one of the most essential functions of police work. Why?

    a. It _____ the work you did.

    b. It creates a _____ of what occurred.

    c. It will be _____ by others who read it.

    d. People will _____ by the quality of your reports.

2. Who is going to read and rely on your reports?

    a. _____

    b. Other officers

    c. Detectives

    d. Prosecutor

    e. Defense attorney

    f. _____

    g. _____

    h. _____

    i. Suspects

    j. _____

    k. _____

    l. _____

    m. _____

   n. News media

   o. _____

3. What are the four prongs that make up a good report?

   a. _____

   b. _____

   c. _____

   d. _____

Make Your Report CLEAR

1. Write _____.

   a. _____ unless your cursive is very legible.

   b. If your handwriting is very bad, use _____ letters.

OR Type

   c. Use 12 or 14 _____ type and a common _____.

   d. (Do) (Do not) use all caps (circle one).

   e. _____-space, _____ between paragraphs.

2. Use proper _____.

   a. Ask people to correctly spell their _____.

   b. Beware of _____ meanings, homonyms, and so on.

   c. Use a _____ or spell-checker

   d. In order to make sure you don't make these mistakes, you should always _____ your report.

3. Write your report _____.

   a. This means in _____ order.

   b. Begin with being _____.

   c. Describe what happened when you arrived.

   d. Specify to whom you spoke.

   e. Tell what you _____ about that individual (if it pertains to the report).

   f. Write what the person _____.

   g. In general, you should _____ the person's statement.

   h. _____ where appropriate.

      i. Be clear about which statements belong to which _____.

      j. Proceed through the interviews, observations, and _____ taken by you.

      k. Conclude the report with a _____.

4. Write in _____ language.

    a. _____ the amount of abbreviations you use. The person reading your report may not be familiar with this abbreviation.

      i. If you do use one, _____ the first time followed by the abbreviation in _____.

    b. Don't _____ use police jargon.

      i. Example: *perp, burg, deuce, collar.* Instead, use: *perpetrator, burglary, DUI, arrest.*

      ii. General police terms are _____ this is a _____ police report.

    c. Don't use slang.

      i. Examples are: *gonna, whack,* and so on.

      ii. Slang is not _____.

      iii. Slang can have different _____ in different regions or social groups.

      iv. Slang usage is _____.

    d. Don't use derogatory terms or profanity. The exception to b, c, and d is when you are _____ someone.

5. Make sure to use proper and best grammar.

    a. Write in the _____ tense. ("I responded to the hospital.")

    b. Write in the _____ person. ("I"; *not* "This officer.")

    c. Write in the _____ voice. ("I arrested Sam. I placed him in handcuffs, searched him, and transported him to jail"; *not* "Sam was arrested by me.")

    d. Avoid run-on sentences.

      i. If you have used the word "_____" a lot in your sentence, it may be a run-on.

    e. Write in _____ sentences.

    f. Change paragraphs when you _____.

6. If you make a mistake . . .
    a. If you are _____, you can hit the _____ key and fix it.
    b. If writing by hand, you may use _____ but you should avoid overuse.
    c. As a last resort, you may _____ with a single line and _____.

7. Using names in a report:
    a. When you first mention someone in your report, mention both their _____ and _____ names.
    b. On subsequent uses, you can refer to the person by _____ his first or his last name.
    c. Using the _____ name sounds more professional.
    d. However, if you have multiple subjects with the same last name, you will have to use either just their _____ names or their _____ names.
    e. Most importantly, be _____ throughout your report in the way that you refer to a particular person. It makes it easier to read and will make more _____ to your reader.

8. There are three options when using numbers in a report.
    a. Write the _____. For example, 8, 12, 68.
    b. Write the _____. For example, eight, twelve, sixty-eight.
    c. Write _____. For example, eight (8), twelve (12), sixty-eight (68).
    d. Referring to time in your police report, you should always use _____ time, except when _____ someone.

9. *Remember:* In order to be of use, your report must be _____.

Make Your Report CONCISE

1. A concise report avoids _____.

2. "Concise" means, very simply, that you should _____.

3. How long should your report be?
    a. Long enough to be _____, _____, and _____.
    b. Don't lose your reader by _____.

4. Anything _____ should be cut out of a report to make it concise.

5. Don't be overly _____ —call a pig a pig.

6. Avoid being _____ (repeating yourself).

7. A concise report reads more _____.

8. A concise report is more _____ (pillar number one).

9. Cut out potato chip _____ like "very."

Make Your Report COMPLETE

1. An important maxim to remember is that if it isn't in the police report, it _____.

2. Make sure that you do the following on every report:

   a. Complete ALL _____.

   b. Include all _____ observations, statements, and actions.

   c. Include all elements of the _____, if applicable.

   d. Check your witness statements:

      i. Whom did you _____ to?

      ii. _____ did you speak with them (or _____ are they related to the call)?

      iii. What did the person _____?

3. How the news reports things:

   a. The five _____ s and the one _____.

   b. W _____ did w _____?

      i. Example: Lucy broke the vase, which belonged to Ricky.

   c. W _____ did it occur (exact time or range)?

   d. W _____ did it occur?

   e. H _____ did it occur?

   f. W _____ did someone do something?

      i. This is the most likely point to be _____.

      ii. Be _____ when answering this question. You may report the opinions of witnesses but ask them to _____.

    iii. Example: Ricky said he thought Lucy broke the vase because she was jealous of his mother. I asked him why he thought this. He said that right before breaking the vase, Lucy said, "You love your mother more than me!"

  g. The police report is often considered the "_____" of an event. This means that third parties will often rely on it as the ultimate authority for what occurred.

Make Your Report ACCURATE

1. It is absolutely _____ that a police report be accurate.

2. Write reports in a _____ manner.

  a. Memory _____, so take good notes.

3. Don't _____.

4. Be _____ and describe things in _____. For example, don't just say "driving recklessly." Describe speed, lane changes, near collisions, and so on.

5. Make _____es / _____s, and _____s be specific during the interview. For example, don't let someone get away with simply saying, "We got into a fight." Get him to describe whether it was physical or verbal, what was said, and what actions were taken.

6. Always _____ your source. Did you observe it or was it reported to you? By whom?

7. Accurately completing biographical information (filling in the boxes) helps your agency and others with regard to _____.

8. It is important to accurately reflect what _____ a person plays in your report.

9. Specify quotes versus paraphrase.

  a. _____ accurately.

  b. _____ exactly.

  c. If you didn't write the quotation down and aren't sure, you can _____ the quotation.

    i. For example: Pete said something similar to "I should be in the damn Hall of Fame."

10. Estimate damage and/or value.

    a. Use _____.

    b. Accept victim's _____—unless it's ridiculous.

    c. If you have personal knowledge or _____ that is relevant, you may use it.

    d. Use _____ to help (NADA guide, etc.).

11. Putting opinions in a police report:

    a. The primary purpose of a police report is to gather and report _____.

    b. There may be a place in your report for a _____ opinion.

    c. Another word for "opinion" in this context might be a _____, supported _____.

    d. If you are including such an opinion, you should:

       i. Avoid _____. For example, "Darnell is black and probably a gang member."

       ii. Avoid _____. For example, "He is living an alternative lifestyle."

    e. If you are considering describing an opinion, be certain there is a logical need for it. One reason for such a need is if you took further _____ as a result of the conclusion you reached.

    f. If you include an opinion/conclusion, be clear that:

       i. You are stating an _____,

       ii. that it is _____ opinion, and

       iii. you list the concrete _____ why you have formed that opinion.

    g. Your opinion must be _____.

       i. For example: "Based upon (1) physical evidence; (2) consistent statements by three independent witnesses; (3) four separate, inconsistent statements made by Suspect Hall; and (4) Hall's mannerisms and behavior during questioning, I _____ that Hall was being untruthful regarding this incident"; *not* "It is my professional opinion that Hall is a _____."

12. A _____ paragraph at the end of a report capsulates events and ensures that the reader accurately understands what has occurred.

13. When you have completed your report, you must _____!

    a. Check for _____ and _____ errors.

    b. Check for _____—does it make sense?

    c. Read _____. It will sound different than when you read silently and you will catch errors you might otherwise miss.

    d. Have _____ read it. That person may catch things you missed or didn't know.

    e. Proofreading also gives you a chance to _____ your report one last time.

Summary

1. So, what elements make a good police report?

    a. It is C _____,

    b. it is C _____,

    c. it is C _____,

    d. and it is A _____.

APPENDIX D

Final Review Key

Here are the answers. Hope you didn't cheat!

Actually, don't sweat this exercise overmuch. If you didn't write the same exact word as the answer that is listed but your word fit the same concept, that is good enough in most cases. Most of this book is conceptual in nature, anyway. You're going to have to take the lessons and make them your own, applying them to your individual set of circumstances every time you sit down to write a report. If you have a specific question, you probably won't be able to look within these pages to find the exact answer. You should be able to find the right concept or framework, though, that will lead you to the correct answer in your individual case.

All that said, here are the correct answers.

Introduction

1. Report writing is one of the most essential functions of police work. Why?
   a. It **DOCUMENTS** the work you did.
   b. It creates a **RECORD** of what occurred.
   c. It will be **RELIED UPON** by others who read it.
   d. People will **JUDGE YOU AND YOUR POLICE WORK** by the quality of your reports.
2. Who is going to read and rely on your reports?
   a. **SUPERVISORS**
   b. Other Officers
   c. Detectives
   d. Prosecutor
   e. Defense Attorney
   f. **CRIME ANALYSIS/CASE SCREENING**
   g. **SOCIAL WORKERS**
   h. **INSURANCE COMPANIES**
   i. Suspects
   j. **PAROLE/PROBATIONS**

   k. **POLICE BRASS**
   l. **INTERNAL AFFAIRS**
   m. **VICTIMS**
   n. News Media
   o. **YOU (LATER IN COURT)**
3. What are the four prongs that make up a good report?
   a. **CLEAR**
   b. **CONCISE**
   c. **COMPLETE**
   d. **ACCURATE**

Make Your Report CLEAR

1. Write **NEATLY**.
   a. **PRINT** unless your cursive is very legible.
   b. If your handwriting is very bad, use **BLOCK** letters.

OR Type

   c. Use 12 or 14 **POINT** type and a common **FONT**.
   d. (Do) / (**DO NOT**) use all caps (circle one).
   e. **SINGLE**-space, **DOUBLE-SPACE** between paragraphs.
2. Use proper **SPELLING**.
   a. Ask people to correctly spell their **NAMES**.
   b. Beware of **MULTIPLE** meanings, homonyms, and so on.
   c. Use a **DICTIONARY** or spell-checker
   d. In order to make sure you don't make these mistakes, you should always **PROOFREAD** your report.
3. Write your report **CHRONOLOGICALLY**.
   a. This means in **TIME** order.
   b. Begin with being **DISPATCHED**.
   c. Describe what happened when you arrived.
   d. Specify to whom you spoke.
   e. Tell what you **OBSERVED** about that individual (if it pertains to the report).
   f. What the person **SAID**.
      i. In general, you should **PARAPHRASE** the person's statement.
      ii. **QUOTE** where appropriate.
   g. Be clear about which statements belong to which **PERSON**.
   h. Proceed through the interviews, observations, and **ACTIONS** taken by you.
   i. Conclude the report with a **DISPOSITION**.

4. Write in **PLAIN** language.
   a. **LIMIT** the amount of abbreviations you use. The person reading your report may not be familiar with this abbreviation.
      i. If you do use one, **WRITE IT OUT** the first time followed by the abbreviation in **PARENTHESES**.
   b. Don't **OVER** use police jargon.
      i. Example: *perp, burg, deuce, collar.* Instead, use: *perpetrator, burglary, DUI, arrest.*
      ii. General police terms are **ACCEPTABLE**—this is a **TECHNICAL** police report
   c. Don't use slang.
      i. Examples are: *gonna, whack,* and so on.
      ii. Slang is not **PROFESSIONAL**.
      iii. Slang can have different **MEANINGS OR USES** in different regions or social groups.
      iv. Slang usage is **SHORT-LIVED**.
   d. Don't use derogatory terms or profanity. The exception to b, c, and d is when you are **QUOTING** someone.
5. Make sure to use proper and best grammar.
   a. Write in the **PAST** tense. ("I responded to the hospital.")
   b. Write in the **FIRST** person. ("I", not "This officer.")
   c. Write in the **ACTIVE** voice. ("I arrested Sam. I placed him in handcuffs, searched him, and transported him to jail"; *not* "Sam was arrested by me.")
   d. Avoid run-on sentences.
      i. If you have used the word "**AND**" a lot in your sentence, it may be a run-on.
   e. Write in **COMPLETE** sentences.
   f. Change paragraphs when you **CHANGE TOPICS**.
6. If you make a mistake. . .
   a. If you are **TYPING**, you can hit the **BACKSPACE** key and fix it.
   b. If writing by hand, you may use **WITE-OUT** but you should avoid overuse.
   c. As a last resort, you may **STRIKE OUT** with a single line and **INITIAL**.
7. Using names in a report:
   a. When you first mention someone in your report, mention both their **FIRST** and **LAST** names.
   b. On subsequent uses, you can refer to the person by **EITHER** his first or his last name.
   c. Using the **LAST** name sounds more professional.
   d. However, if you have multiple subjects with the same last name, you will have to use either just their **FIRST** names or their **COMPLETE** names.

    e. Most importantly, be **CONSISTENT** throughout your report in the way that you refer to a particular person. It makes it easier to read and will make more **SENSE** to your reader.

8. There are three options when using numbers in a report.
   a. Write the **NUMERAL**. For example, 8, 12, 68.
   b. Write the **WORD**. For example, eight, twelve, sixty-eight.
   c. Write **BOTH**. For example, eight (8), twelve (12), sixty-eight (68).
   d. Referring to time in your police report, you should always use **MILITARY** time, except when **QUOTING** someone.

9. *Remember:* In order to be of use, your report must be **CLEAR**.

Make Your Report CONCISE

1. A concise report avoids **CLUTTER**.
2. "Concise" means, very simply, that you should **GET TO THE POINT**.
3. How long should your report be?
   a. Long enough to be **CLEAR**, **COMPLETE**, and **ACCURATE**.
   b. Don't lose your reader by **OVERWRITING**.
4. Anything **UNNECESSARY** should be cut out of a report to make it concise.
5. Don't be overly **VERBOSE**—call a pig a pig.
6. Avoid being **REDUNDANT** (repeating yourself).
7. A concise report reads more **PROFESSIONALLY**.
8. A concise report is more **CLEAR** (pillar number one).
9. Cut out potato chip **WORDS** like "very."

Make Your Report COMPLETE

1. An important maxim to remember is that if it isn't in the police report, it **DIDN'T HAPPEN**.
2. Make sure that you do the following on every report:
   a. Complete ALL **BOXES**.
   b. Include all **RELEVANT** observations, statements, and actions.
   c. Include all elements of the **CRIME**, if applicable.
   d. Check your witness statements:
      i. Whom did you **SPEAK** to?
      ii. **WHY** did you speak with them (or **HOW** are they related to the call)?
      iii. What did the person **SAY**?
3. How the news reports things:
   a. The five **W**s and the one **H**.
   b. W**HO** did w**HAT**?
      i. Example: Lucy broke the vase, which belonged to Ricky
   c. W**HEN** did it occur (exact time or range)?

    d. W**HERE** did it occur?

    e. H**OW** it occurred.

    f. W**HY** did someone do something?

       i. This is the most likely point to be **UNKNOWN**.

      ii. Be **CAREFUL** when answering this question. You may report the opinions of witnesses but ask them to **CLARIFY**.

     iii. Example: Ricky said he thought Lucy broke the vase because she was jealous of his mother. I asked him why he thought this. He said that right before breaking the vase, Lucy said, "You love your mother more than me!"

4. The police report is often considered the "**BIBLE**" of an event. This means that third parties will often rely on it as the ultimate authority for what occurred.

Make Your Report ACCURATE

1. It is absolutely **CRITICAL** that a police report be accurate.

2. Write reports in a **TIMELY** manner.

    a. Memory **FADES**, so take good notes.

3. Don't **ASSUME**.

4. Be **SPECIFIC** and describe things in **DETAIL**. For example, don't just say "driving recklessly." Describe speed, lane changes, near collisions, and so on.

5. Make **WITNESS**es / **VICTIM**s, and **SUSPECT**s be specific during the interview. For example, don't let someone get away with simply saying, "We got into a fight." Get him to describe whether it was physical or verbal, what was said, and what actions were taken.

6. Always **CITE** your source. Did you observe it or was it reported to you? By whom?

7. Accurately completing biographical information (filling in the boxes) helps your agency and others with regard to **CRIMINAL INTELLIGENCE**.

8. It is important to accurately reflect what **ROLE** a person plays in your report.

9. Specify quotes versus paraphrase.

    a. **PARAPHRASE** accurately.

    b. **QUOTE** exactly.

    c. If you didn't write the quotation down and aren't sure, you can **QUALIFY** the quotation.

       i. For example: Pete said something similar to "I should be in the damn Hall of Fame."

10. Estimate damage and/or value.

    a. Use **COMMON SENSE**.

    b. Accept victim's **ESTIMATE**—unless it's ridiculous.

    c. If you have personal knowledge or **EXPERIENCE** that is relevant, you may use it.

    d. Use **RESOURCES** to help (NADA guide, etc.).

11. Putting opinions in a police report:
    a. The primary purpose of a police report is to gather and report **FACTS**.
    b. There may be a place in your report for a **PROFESSIONAL** opinion.
    c. Another word for "opinion" in this context might be a **PROFESSIONAL**, supported **CONCLUSION**.
    d. If you are including such an opinion, you should:
        i. Avoid **PREJUDICE/STEREOTYPES**. For example, "Darnell is black and probably a gang member."
        ii. Avoid **EUPHEMISMS**. For example, "He is living an alternative lifestyle."
    e. If you are considering describing an opinion, be certain there is a logical need for it. One reason for such a need is if you took further **ACTION** as a result of the conclusion you reached.
    f. If you include an opinion/conclusion, be clear that:
        i. You are stating an **OPINION**,
        ii. that it is **YOUR** opinion, and
        iii. you list the concrete **REASONS** why you have formed that opinion.
    g. Your opinion must be **PROFESSIONAL**.
        i. For example: "Based upon (1) physical evidence; (2) consistent statements by three independent witnesses; (3) four separate, inconsistent statements made by Suspect Hall; and (4) Hall's mannerisms and behavior during questioning, I **CONCLUDED** that Hall was being untruthful regarding this incident"; *not* "It is my professional opinion that Hall is a **LIAR**."
12. A **SUMMARIZING** paragraph at the end of a report capsulates events and ensures that the reader accurately understands what has occurred.
13. When you have completed your report, you must **PROOFREAD**!
    a. Check for **SPELLING** and **GRAMMAR** errors.
    b. Check for **CONTENT**—does it make sense?
    c. Read **ALOUD**. It will sound different than when you read silently and you will catch errors you might otherwise miss.
    d. Have **SOMEONE ELSE** read it. That person may catch things you missed or didn't know.
    e. Proofreading also gives you a chance to **REVISE** your report one last time.

Summary

1. So, what elements make a good police report?
    a. It is **CLEAR**,
    b. it is **CONCISE**,
    c. it is **COMPLETE**,
    d. and it is **ACCURATE**.

APPENDIX E

A (Good) Example Burglary Report

When you've finished with your five stages of revising the example provided in chapter four, your report should look something along the lines of the report that follows.

The five stages you should have gone through were to (1–4) revise for clarity, conciseness, completeness, and accuracy and to (5) proofread the final revision.

See how you compare. Remember, yours doesn't need to be exactly the same, but it should be similar in those important elements.

> On 020712 at approx. 1530 hours, I responded to 2914 E Indiana on a report of a residential burglary.
>
> Upon arrival, I contacted the complainant/victim, Susannah Rettinghouse, who told me the following:
>
> She and her husband, Brian Rettinghouse, had left their home on 020512 at approx. 1500 hours to attend a wedding in Ellensburg, Washington. She believed the house was locked up when they had left. She returned alone on 020712 at approx. 1115 hours. She parked her car in the garage and entered the house through the entry door leading from the garage into the kitchen.
>
> She immediately noticed her cabinet doors and drawers were standing open in the kitchen. She also saw the rear sliding glass door was standing open. She called 911 and then began looking through the house for missing items.
>
> She discovered the dresser drawers in the master bedroom had been ransacked. The only thing she found missing was $1,570.00 she had hidden in one of

the drawers. She looked through the rest of the house and couldn't find anything else missing or disturbed. All of the other doors and windows were still locked.

I looked at the sliding glass door for evidence of damage but was unable to locate any. Susannah told me her teenage son, Jeffery Rettinghouse, sometimes forgets to lock the door. She said she didn't know where he was at that time but mentioned he had stayed in Spokane with her parents that weekend. She said her parents only live a few blocks away. She said Jeffery had been in trouble recently for taking things that didn't belong to him. She was unsure whether Jeffery would have committed this crime.

While standing in the kitchen area, Susannah pointed to an empty Pepsi pop can on her kitchen counter and stated it hadn't been there when they had left. The refrigerator had several Pepsi pop cans inside of it.

I photographed the empty Pepsi can and ransacked bedroom. I was unable to locate any fingerprints on the point of entry/exit or on the dresser drawers.

I went next door and spoke to the male neighbor, John James, who told me the following:

He had heard a noise next door on 020612 in the early afternoon. He looked over and saw a teenaged male walking in the backyard of the house. He watched the male for a few moments but didn't say anything because he assumed it was the boy who lived there. He didn't see if the male had entered the house.

I gave Susannah a crime victim card with the incident number on it. I asked her to call detectives if she discovered anything else missing.

I collected the Pepsi can as evidence and put it on property as evidence. A request for prints was completed and submitted with the Pepsi can.

Case referred to detectives for follow-up.

Officer Strosahl #565

INDEX